Southern Steam Revival

Introduction

D1494635

Southern steam did not die completely in July 1967; one railway was keeping it going and much has since been achieved since the early success of the Bluebell Railway.

The 'Bournemouth Belle', the 'Golden Arrow', the 'Night Ferry' and the 'Atlantic Coast Express', green coaches, Eastleigh works, Clapham Junction, Honiton bank, Dover Marine, Brighton 'Terriers', Adams 'Radials' and of course Bulleid Pacifics; this is how the Southern Railway and later the Southern Region of British Railways is remembered. And it is not just memories; the railway preservation movement has created some remarkable reincarnations of the glory days of Southern steam, ranging from an immaculate Merchant Navy on a rake of Pullmans to a Beattie well tank on a china clay train in Cornwall. It has been a long time since the Bluebell Railway ran its first trains with a couple of 0-6-0Ts but the heritage lines go from strength to strength while main line steam on Southern metals has become a regular occurrence in recent times.

The Southern Railway was an amalgamation mainly of the South Eastern & Chatham Railway, London Brighton & South Coast Railway and London & South Western Railway. A large part of its business was commuter and much of the network had already been electrified by 1923, still more by 1948, and this was continued by the Southern Region of British Railways.

But there were still rural branch lines, cross-country routes and long-distance main lines, to the west at least, during Southern Railway days. The make-up of the SR system led to the survival of some relatively old classes of steam engine.

Many classes comprised fairly small numbers of engines, there were relatively few express engines and very few heavy goods types. But what transformed the SR motive power scene was the arrival of Oliver Bulleid as chief mechanical engineer in 1937. Despite the war, the SR belatedly found itself with 140 of the most free-steaming, modern, powerful express engines ever to have run in Britain. In BR days, with further major electrification projects completed in the late 1950s, the Bulleid Pacifics could handle most of the SR's express workings and a lot more besides, supplemented by many BR Standard 4-6-0s, and as a result the older express classes were early casualties.

The story of SR steam in its last days in the early to mid-1960s saw some remarkable survivors though, such as the Beattie well tanks, Brighton 'Terriers', SECR O1s, the Adams Radial 4-4-2Ts and of course the Isle of Wight O2s, while the Bulleids lasted right up to electrification to Bournemouth in 1967.

The revival of Southern steam in the preservation era has been shaped by the fortunes of the major heritage railways and by British Railways' policy. While the first preserved standard gauge preserved railway was the Bluebell, deep in Southern territory, opening in 1960, followed by the Kent & East Sussex Railway and the Isle of Wight Steam Railway, other preservation schemes in the south seemed to founder, and the two other major lines which we now associate with Southern steam preservation, the Mid-Hants Railway and the Swanage Railway, were relative latecomers, not opening until 1977, and the late 1980s respectively.

Meanwhile the electrification of such a significant proportion of the SR main line system resulted in virtually no main line steam action on the region throughout the 1970s and much of the 1980s. Merchant Navy Pacific No. 35028 *Clan Line* managed one trip in non-electrified territory from Eastleigh to Westbury in 1974, but it was not repeated and it was not until 1986 that steam was finally allowed on the SR again albeit only on the 42-mile run between Salisbury and Yeovil Junction.

In the meantime, active Southern steam was in many cases often seen far away from home territory. No. 35028 was based at Hereford and regularly ran to points even further north, while many heritage lines north of the Thames were graced by examples of Southern steam power. The National Collection's two express 4-6-0s No. 777 *Sir Lamiel* and No. 850 *Lord Nelson* were very much northern-based engines, and in fact the sole Bulleid Pacific active on the Southern for many years was West Country 21C123 *Blackmoor Vale* on the Bluebell, until the Mid-Hants and Swanage railways opened for business.

The real main line breakthrough on the Southern did not come until 1992 when Severn Valley-based rebuilt West Country Pacific No. 34027 *Taw Valley* ran from Waterloo to Bournemouth after dark. This was eventually permitted in daylight from 1994 and the MHR took the plunge into main line running with its Daylight Railtours programme from 1998 using its own set of green stock, followed in 2000 by Steam Dreams' even more ambitious 'Cathedrals Express' venture.

Privatisation of the main line network really opened the floodgates for main line steam on the Southern, and steam is almost an everyday sight on the main line in the 21st century. *Clan Line* spearheaded the use of air brakes on preserved steam locomotives, and became a familiar sight on the Venice Simplon Orient-Express Pullmans.

The reconnection of the Bluebell Railway to the main line network in 2013 means that all three major lines have a main line connection, and while this has been the principal reconstruction project to have taken place, other major extensions are in progress, while more locomotives are under restoration and the Southern steam revival maintains its momentum.

Eighty-nine steam locomotives of the Southern Railway or its constituent companies' designs survive in preservation; this publication traces in detail the history of each of them.

Editor:
Brian Sharpe

Designer:
Tim Pipes

Reprographics:
Jonathan Schofield & Lorna Herbert

Senior sub-editor:
Dan Sharp

Production manager:
Craig Lamb

Publisher:
Tim Hartley

Publishing director:
Dan Savage

Commercial director:
Nigel Hole

Published by:
Mortons Media Group Ltd,
Media Centre,
Morton Way,
Horncastle,
Lincolnshire
LN9 6JR
Tel: 01507 529529

ISBN:
978-1-909128-45-3

Medstead & Four Marks signalbox on the Mid-Hants Railway.

COVER IMAGE
MAIN IMAGE: Bulleid Pacifics No. 34072 *257 Squadron* and No. 34105 *Swanage* accelerate away from Swanage on March 19, 1993.

ABOVE: Corfe Castle station on the Swanage Railway.

TOP: LBSCR A1X 0-6-0T No. 32636 passes under Three Arch Bridge on the Bluebell Railway on February 25, 1989.

RIGHT: LSWR T9 4-4-0 No. 30120 and West Country Pacific No. 34016 *Bodmin* at Ropley on the Mid-Hants Railway.

Contents

3	Introduction
6	Southern Heritage Lines
12	The National Collection
14	Southern Locomotives
16	Southern Main Line Steam
18	South Eastern & Chatham Railway
20	O1 0-6-0 No. 65
22	C class 0-6-0 No. 592
23	H class 0-4-4T No. 263
24	P class 0-6-0T
26	London Brighton & South Coast Railway
28	A1 and A1X class 0-6-0T 'Terriers'
32	E1 0-6-0T No. 110 *Burgundy* and E4 0-6-2T No. 473 *Birch Grove*
34	H2 4-4-2 No. 32424 *Beachy Head*
36	London & South Western Railway
38	0298 class 2-4-0WT
40	Adams Radial 415 class 4-4-2T No. 488 and O2 0-4-4T W24 *Calbourne*
42	B4 0-4-0T
43	M7 0-4-4T
46	T9 4-4-0 No. 120
48	L&B 2-6-2T No. 190 *Lyd*
50	LSWR S15 4-6-0
52	The Southern Railway
54	SR S15 4-6-0
58	King Arthur 4-6-0 No. 777 *Sir Lamiel*
62	N class 2-6-0
63	U class 2-6-0
66	Schools class 4-4-0
70	Lord Nelson 4-6-0 No. 850 *Lord Nelson*
73	Q class 0-6-0 No. 541
74	USA class 0-6-0T
78	Oliver Bulleid
80	Bulleid Pacifics
82	West Country Pacific No. 34007 *Wadebridge*
84	West Country Pacific No. 21C123 *Blackmore Vale*

86	Battle of Britain No. 34067 *Tangmere* and No. 34051 *Winston Churchill*
90	Battle of Britain Pacifics No. 34070 *Manston,* No. 34072 *257 Squadron* and No. 34073 *249 Squadron*
94	Battle of Britain Pacific No. 34081 *92 Squadron*
96	West Country Pacific No. 34092 *City of Wells*
98	West Country Pacific No. 34105 *Swanage*
100	Rebuilding of the Bulleid Pacifics West Country Pacific No. 34010 *Sidmouth*
102	West Country Pacific No. 34016 *Bodmin*
104	West Country Pacific No. 34027 *Taw Valley*
108	West Country Pacifics No. 34028 *Eddystone,* No. 34039 *Boscastle* and No. 34010 *Sidmouth*
110	Battle of Britain Pacifics No. 34053 *Sir Keith Park,* No. 34058 *Sir Frederick Pile* and No. 34059 *Sir Archibald Sinclair*
112	West Country No. 34046 *Braunton*
115	West Country No. 34101 *Hartland*
116	Merchant Navy Pacific No. 35005 *Canadian Pacific*
118	Merchant Navy Pacifics No. 35006 *Peninsular & Oriental S N Co,* No. 35009 *Shaw Savill,* No. 35010 *Blue Star,* No. 35011 *General Steam Navigation* and No. 35018 *British India Line.*
120	Merchant Navy Pacifics No. 35027 *Port Line,* No. 35022 *Holland-America Line* and No. 35025 *Brocklebank Line.*
124	Merchant Navy No. 35028 *Clan Line*
128	Merchant Navy Pacific No. 35029 *Ellerman Lines*
130	Southern Steam Revival: The Future

Merchant Navy Pacific No. 35005 *Canadian Pacific,* Battle of Britain No. 34070 *Manston* and West Country No. 34028 *Eddystone* at Eastleigh works during an open weekend in May 2009.

CHAPTER 1

Southern Heritage Lines

From the pioneering Bluebell Railway and the Kent & East Sussex and Isle of Wight Steam railways, through the failed schemes at Longmoor, Westerham and Droxford, to the Swanage and Mid-Hants railways, and the re-creation of the Lynton & Barnstaple Railway.

The Bluebell Railway, the first standard gauge preserved steam railway in Britain, carried the flag for Southern preserved steam throughout the 1960s. The only other successful schemes in the south until the late 1970s were the Kent & East Sussex Railway and Isle of Wight Steam Railways, while schemes launched at Westerham and Droxford foundered. A steam centre was established at Ashford, but the hope for big Southern steam briefly centred round the Longmoor Military Railway in Hampshire, which offered potential as both a heritage line in its own right and a main line operating base. But it was not to be; Ashford closed, while Longmoor never got off the ground.

While the Bluebell was essentially a five-mile branch line, using small engines which outgrew its potential, the two major heritage lines which offered opportunities for big steam did not run trains until the late 1970s; the Mid-Hants and Swanage railways.

The 2ft gauge Lynton & Barnstaple Railway had closed in the 1930s, but saw a remarkable revival in the 21st century, while the Bluebell Railway reached East Grinstead and the main line in 2013, re-establishing itself as a market leader.

BLUEBELL RAILWAY

The Bluebell Railway was the first standard gauge preserved railway in Britain to run regular steam-hauled passenger services, initially from Sheffield Park station to a point just south of Horsted Keynes. March 2013 saw the railway finally complete its extension to Horsted Keynes, to link it with the national network once again for the first time since 1963.

In 1954, long before the Beeching axe, the BR's branch line committee proposed closing the LBSCR line from East Grinstead to Culver Junction, near Lewes. This was challenged by local residents, but closure was agreed for June 15, 1955; however, an acrimonious battle between British Railways and the users of the Bluebell Line lasted three years. The users initially met with success and got the line reopened until it was finally closed on March 17, 1958.

On March 15, 1959, a group met in Ardingly and formed the Lewes and East Grinstead Railway Preservation Society. A total of £940 was raised through donations to start the society, which later changed its name to the Bluebell Railway Preservation Society, its initial aim being to reopen the whole line as a commercial service, using a two-car DMU. This met with no success, but plan B was that the line between Sheffield Park and Horsted Keynes could be run as a tourist attraction, with vintage locomotives and stock operated by unpaid amateur staff, as had been done by the narrow gauge Talyllyn Railway in Wales.

BR still ran an electrified line from East Grinstead to Ardingly through Horsted Keynes, and in 1960 the line was opened from Sheffield Park to Bluebell Halt, 100 yards south of Horsted Keynes.

In 1974, the society took the first steps towards an extension north to East Grinstead, and bought the freehold of the site of Kingscote station in January 1985. After a public enquiry, planning permission and a Light Railway Order for an extension to East Grinstead were granted in 1985. The extension from Horsted Keynes to Kingscote was completed in 1994, and trains once again ran right through to East Grinstead from March 2013, giving a total line length of 11 miles.

Stepney **hauls the inaugural train on the Bluebell Railway at Sheffield Park in August 1960.** BLUEBELL ARCHIVE

KENT & EAST SUSSEX RAILWAY

Tenterden in Kent was in the middle of a triangle of railway lines, but with the passing of the Light Railways Act 1896, a group of Tenterden citizens led by Sir Myles Fenton proposed a railway from Robertsbridge to Tenterden – the Rother Valley Railway. The work was overseen by Holman F Stephens, who was appointed managing director in 1900.

An associate member of the Institution of Civil Engineers, he could design and build railways in his own right, and had embarked on his lifetime's project of building light railways for rural areas, which was to total 16 – many of these stayed independent of the larger systems created by Grouping in 1923. The line was opened to passenger traffic on April 2, 1900.

A section from the original Tenterden terminus to Tenterden Town was opened on April 15, 1903, and the original Tenterden station was renamed Rolvenden. The RVR built and operated the line from Tenterden to Headcorn, and in 1904 changed its name to the Kent & East Sussex Light Railway.

The K&ESR was not included in the Grouping of the railways into the 'Big Four' in 1923, and continued its independent existence, but by 1924 was operating at a loss, and became part of

BR, Southern Region on Nationalisation.

Regular passenger services ceased and the final passenger train ran on January 2, 1954: the 5.50pm from Robertsbridge to Headcorn, with 'Terrier' 0-6-0Ts Nos. 32655 leading and 32678 at the rear.

A service of two freight trains a day continued, with hop-pickers' specials running until 1958, and the final passenger train over the line before closure was a Locomotive Club of Great Britain railtour on June 11, 1961.

Although a preservation scheme was launched immediately, difficulties in obtaining the necessary Light Railway (Transfer) Order meant it was 1974 before the line reopened between Tenterden and Rolvenden, extended to Wittersham Road in 1977 and Northiam in 1990. The most recent extension was to Bodiam, opened in 2000.

The preserved line currently runs a total distance of 11½ miles, but has suffered from the legacy of Colonel Stephens' method of cheap and poor construction. This has meant updating permanent way features such as renewal of culverts and embankments to allow the use of much larger locomotives.

A1X 0-6-0T No. 10 *Sutton* at Rolvenden on the occasion of the official reopening of the Kent & East Sussex Railway on June 1, 1974. The Rt Hon William Deedes, MP for Ashford, performed the official ceremony. JOHN TITLOW

ISLE OF WIGHT STEAM RAILWAY

The five-mile steam railway and an electrified eight-mile main line from Ryde to Shanklin are all that remains of a railway system on the island, which totalled 55 miles by 1900. The Wight Locomotive Society was launched by Ron Strutt and Iain Whitlam to try to preserve at least one LSWR O2 0-4-4T, and possibly a carriage or two, when steam services ended on December 31, 1966.

An organisation called Vectrail formulated plans for the lines that closed at this time. It came to nothing, but bought a bit of time for the WLS to become established.

A budding wildlife artist called David Shepherd put £500 into the WLS funds, pushing the total much nearer the £900 required, so that No. 24 *Calbourne*, two SECR coaches, and three LBSCR ones were bought.

The society needed a short piece of line on which to store and possibly operate its collection, and in 1969 the engine was moved by road from Ryde to join its train at Newport (although the new base was to be at Havenstreet), enough money having been raised to pay the deposit on 1⅝ mile of line from Wootton to Havenstreet.

Calbourne actually steamed to Havenstreet with its train in October 1971, and the first passenger trains ran the following Easter, over a mile of track towards Wootton, although it was not until 1986 that the new station was opened at Wootton.

The railway subsequently extended eastwards, reaching

Smallbrook Junction by 1991, where an interchange platform was built by BR Island Line for cross-platform access to trains on the Ryde to Shanklin line.

ISLE OF WIGHT STEAM RAILWAY

On the first day of operations on the Isle of Wight Steam Railway, LSWR O2 0-4-4T No. 24 *Calbourne* operates in push-pull fashion at Havenstreet on April 12 1972. RICHARD J NEWMAN

Bulleid Pacifics Nos. 34023
Blackmoor Vale and 35028
Clan Line stored at
Longmoor on May 19, 1968.
COLOUR-RAIL.COM

LONGMOOR MILITARY RAILWAY

An 18in gauge tramway was built by the Royal Engineers from 1903 to train soldiers on railway construction and operations. It was relaid to standard gauge in 1905/1907 and was renamed the Longmoor Military Railway in 1935, having been extended to Liss in 1933.

A passenger service was operated, nominally for railway personnel, but withdrawn on September 16, 1957. Although closed, the original line to Bordon remained in place – while there was a BR connection at Liss, the Bordon branch made it easier to move military traffic at short notice. In 1966, though, traffic on the Bordon branch was suspended, and the line was lifted in 1967.

In light of the smaller role of the military and the severely reduced British Empire, it was decided by the Ministry of Defence to close the railway. The small, but complete, rail system would have made an instant heritage railway, with potential as a main line operating base for the south of England, but the MoD

rejected the proposal, offering only the last 1½ miles of line from Liss Forest Road to Liss. The offer was accepted, and a revised plan was progressed.

Although it would be nothing like that originally envisaged, the LMR was seen as the centre for big Southern steam preservation. Bulleid Pacifics Nos. 35028 *Clan Line* and 34023 *Blackmore Vale*, USA 0-6-0T No. 30064, and other locomotives – including David Shepherd's two BR Standards, No. 92203 *Black Prince* and No. 75029 *The Green Knight* – took up residence in the meantime.

Unfortunately, the people of Liss opposed the planning proposal, and a consortium of residents raised £9100 in a successful bid to buy this last piece of line.

The LMR closed down with a ceremonial last day of operation on October 31, 1969, with the remaining locomotives being moved away over the next couple of years.

WESTERHAM VALLEY RAILWAY

The Westerham Valley Railway ran for 4½ miles from Dunton Green, on the SECR main line, to Westerham in Kent. It closed on October 28, 1961.

In 1962, the Westerham Valley Railway Association proposed reopening the line, staffed by volunteers, for commuters on weekdays and as a heritage railway at weekends. In July 1962, BR granted a lease of Westerham station building,

However, BR policy regarding the disposal of disused branch lines kept changing, partly through interest being shown by the council in using land for the Sevenoaks bypass, and proposals for the M25 motorway, and it wanted to sell outright. Thanks to the help of an anonymous backer, the association was able to make an offer of £30,000 for the track, buildings, land and branch platform at Dunton Green, but the withdrawal of the backer following the refusal of his planning application to develop land at Westerham station cast serious doubt on the project.

In the meantime, the purchase of several former Metropolitan Railway coaches and SECR H class 0-4-4T No. 31263 had been agreed. Initially, BR had allowed the stock to be stored at Dunton Green, but since the intervention of Kent County Council, it became 'reluctant' to allow this, and threatened to scrap it if not collected.

Unless the association could come up with the cost of constructing a bridge over the railway cutting at Chevening, to enable the Sevenoaks bypass to cross it, the project was doomed. It was clearly impossible, and in autumn 1965 the association merged with the Kent & East Sussex Railway Preservation Society.

By March 1967, the railway track had been lifted and Westerham station demolished. Work on the section of the M25 from Sundridge Road to Westerham started in December 1976 and was completed three years later.

MEON VALLEY RAILWAY

The Meon Valley line ran between Alton and Fareham. It opened in 1903, making it one of the last main line railways of any size to be built in the UK.

After closure of the southern portion of the line in 1962, Charles Ashby bought Droxford station and the right to run trains. He used it for testing a design of railbus called the Sadler Rail Coach. A company called Sadler Vectrail Ltd was established in 1966 to reopen the Ryde to Cowes railway on the Isle of Wight, using Sadler Rail Coaches.

Ashby also bought a LBSCR A1X 'Terrier' 0-6-0T No. 32646, which he brought to Droxford, but in May 1966 this was sold to

Brickwoods, the Portsmouth-based brewer, for use as a pub sign outside a public house on Hayling Island.

The line also became home to a steam locomotive preservation society, which planned to operate it as a preserved railway. Several locomotives, including a USA 0-6-0T No. 30064, as well as rolling stock, were moved to Droxford, but a fire at the site meant that plans came to nothing.

Once the main line connection was gone, Ashby briefly used two industrial diesel shunters and two coaches on private-charter trains. The line south of Wickham was lifted in 1974, and the last remaining section from there to Droxford in 1975.

MID-HANTS RAILWAY

The line from Alton to Winchester was opened on October 2, 1865 as the Mid-Hants Railway, but operated by the LSWR, which eventually bought it in 1884.

It gained its popular name The Watercress Line as it was used to transport locally grown watercress to markets in London.

Often used as a diversionary route for Bournemouth line expresses, it was a main line, although single track with steep gradients. A trip over it was referred to by locomotive crews as going 'over the Alps' as it climbed to a summit 652 feet above sea level near Medstead & Four Marks station.

Electrification of the line as far as Alton in 1937 meant that the line onwards to Winchester lost its regular through trains, and it became a quiet backwater, eventually closing in 1973.

Plans for a preserved railway on the Meon Valley line, which ran south from Alton, had unfortunately floundered, but from the ashes of this scheme rose new plans for the Mid-Hants line westwards from Alton. It was naturally hoped that the entire route could be saved, but it became clear that the proposed Winchester bypass was going to sever the line and the revivalists would have to settle for a western terminus at Alresford.

The preserved Mid-Hants Railway now runs for 10 miles from Alresford to Alton, where it connects to the main line network. It was bought from BR in November 1975 and the first section, between Alresford and Ropley, reopened on April 30, 1977.

The extension to Medstead & Four Marks opened on May 14, 1983, and the final section to Alton on May 25, 1985, after the

track was relaid. Being a late starter in heritage railway terms, but needing big motive power, it has had to rely on ex-Barry scrapyard engines and has become known as a centre for big SR steam engines, particularly Bulleid Pacifics.

Uniquely among the Southern heritage lines, the Mid-Hants Railway upgraded both locomotives and rolling stock to enable it to operate railtours on the national network, using its own trains. Daylight Railtours was highly successful for some years, but it became increasingly difficult for the railway to run the train on to the main line at Alton at agreed times. It was decided to withdraw the service and concentrate on the preserved railway business.

A 1950s Southern steam shed image is re-created at Ropley on the Mid-Hants Railway in the summer of 1987, with LSWR T9 4-4-0 No. 30120, two moguls and a Bulleid Pacific.

Plenty of Southern green in evidence at the Mid-Hants Railway's Alresford station.

LYNTON & BARNSTAPLE RAILWAY

Railways eventually reached Minehead and Ilfracombe, but the heart of Exmoor had much more difficult terrain to overcome, and a railway to Lynton seemed an impossibility. However, construction of the 1ft 11½in gauge Lynton and Barnstaple railway began in 1895.

It was originally equipped with three Manning Wardle 2-6-2Ts named *Yeo, Exe* and *Taw,* and was bought by the Southern Railway in 1923, but it continued to lose money and was closed in 1935.

The railway's rolling stock and track were sold at auction and the locomotives were cut up for scrap, but the trackbed has remained mostly untouched as have some of the bridges; the magnificent Chelfham Viaduct is still standing, silently waiting for trains to return.

Back in 1979, a keen band of volunteers got together to restore this lost railway. But rebuilding the L&B is an extremely ambitious project which few back then would even consider attempting to undertake.

Despite this, great progress has been made in the past few years and today Woody Bay station is restored, having been reopened in 2003, and trains run for a mile to Killington Lane.

In 2011, the Ffestiniog Railway's new-build L&B Manning Wardle 2-6-2T *Lyd* visited and it returned in 2013, together with two newly restored L&B coaches. Rebuilding the whole line will take a very long time – buying the sections of trackbed is a convoluted process, but authentic steam trains are running on a section of the SR which closed in 1935.

As if it were 1935 again: *Lyd* **stands in Woody Bay station in May 2013.** PHIL WATERFIELD

SWANAGE RAILWAY

Bulleid Battle of Britain Pacific No. 34067 *Tangmere* on the 'Royal Wessex' from Victoria, passes No. 34070 *Manston* at Corfe Castle on May 2, 2009. ROBIN JONES

The branch from Wareham to Swanage was built by the Swanage Railway Company. It opened in 1885 and was operated by the LSWR.

Although closure was initially suggested in the 1950s, it was not included in the Beeching report and after BR issued a closure notice for September 1968, it took many years to implement, not closing until January 1972. In May that year, the Swanage Railway Society was formed to operate a year-round service linking to the main line at Wareham, 'subsidised' by steam-hauled trains in summer.

The Swanage Railway follows the route of the old Purbeck branch line from Norden via Corfe Castle, Harmans Cross and Herston Halt to Swanage. In 1979, a short section from Swanage reopened, extended first to Herston Halt and then to Harmans Cross in 1988. In 1995, the railway was reopened from Swanage to Corfe Castle and Norden Park and Ride, a distance of six miles.

Freight traffic had continued on a short section of the branch from Wareham, but eventually ended. On January 3, 2002, the Swanage Railway track was temporarily joined with the Furzebrook freight line at Motala and the line was once again complete, 30 years to the day after it closed.

On September 8 that year, the first main line train ran onto the branch and through to Swanage. On May 10, 2007, the connection with Network Rail had been made permanent and was used for the first time for an incoming stock movement. On May 2, 2009, the first public passenger-carrying steam train since 1967 arrived at Swanage from Victoria behind Battle of Britain Pacific No. 34067 *Tangmere*.

Work is continuing to provide the infrastructure necessary to enable regular services via Wareham to be implemented.

SPA VALLEY RAILWAY

Tunbridge Wells in Kent had two stations built by rival companies; Central, opened in 1845 by the SER, which is now the only main line station, and West, which was opened by the LBSCR in 1866. There were once direct services from Tunbridge Wells West to the South Coast at Brighton and to London Victoria, but it is now the headquarters of Spa Valley Railway.

Tunbridge Wells to Eridge closed on July 6, 1985, the first railway closure in the area since the Beeching cuts of the 1960s.

The Tunbridge Wells and Eridge Railway Preservation Society, commonly referred to as TWERPS, was quickly established to try to reopen the line. After years of hard work, in 1994 the society acquired the line – following a generous loan from Tunbridge Wells Borough Council – and by winter 1996 was running trains on half a mile of track towards Groombridge, having merged with the North

Downs Steam Railway at Dartford, which had closed.

The line was reopened through to Groombridge in August 1997, giving a total length of three and a half miles. Groombridge now has a new station building, a signalbox, and has benefited from other improvements.

The line has continued to progress, and in 2005 opened an extension, which runs just short of the former Birchden Junction, a further mile from Groombridge, on the boundary with the main line. However, the intention remained to extend back to Eridge, a further mile down the line, and this project was finally realised in March 2011.

The line has only rarely seen locomotives of true Southern pedigree, but it is hoped that this will become more commonplace in future.

There are a number of other heritage lines on former SR routes which have seen steam services in operation, though not with SR steam power. In Devon, there is the Dartmoor Railway, between Okehampton and Meldon Quarry, which saw its first steam services in 2001 using a Hunslet 0-6-0ST. It does, however, remain connected to the national network, and has seen ballast trains running from the quarry and even the occasional main line steam railtour. The line has been taken over by an American railroad company, and the future of its services remains unclear.

In Cornwall, the Launceston Steam Railway runs a regular steam service on a new 1ft 11½in gauge line, and the Lavender Line at Isfield, very close to the Bluebell Railway, operates regular passenger services with industrial steam locomotives.

The Col Stephens East Kent Railway has also seen a revival with passenger trains occasionally having industrial steam power. Part of the Seaton branch operates as the 3ft gauge Seaton Tramway, and a steam centre has been set up at Yeovil Junction, where main line engines are regularly serviced.

CHAPTER 2

The National Collection

Even without the contribution made by private enterprise, with invaluable assistance from Dai Woodham, a good representative selection of Southern steam power would still have survived.

Steam preservation in the south started long before the formation of the Southern Railway, with the preservation of Canterbury & Whitstable Railway 0-4-0 *Invicta*. This was the first steam locomotive to transport fare paying passengers on a public railway in Great Britain and the world's first preserved locomotive .

In 1825, the Canterbury & Whitstable Railway became the first railway in the south of England and the first to use steam locomotives. It was purchased in 1853 by the South Eastern Railway. The seven mile line chosen involved steep gradients and several tunnels. George Stephenson was appointed engineer but his son Robert Stephenson supervised the construction work which took four years to complete.

When it opened in 1830, the Canterbury & Whitstable Railway was the first stteam-worked public railway to offer both a passenger and freight service.

Only the last two miles of the route in Whitstable were worked by *Invicta*, which was based on the design of

Stephenson's *Rocket*. Unfortunately though, it was found to be unable to haul trains up the incline from Whitstable Harbour, and a third stationary steam engine was installed.

Inevitably *Invicta* was withdrawn in 1839 and offered for sale, but although there were no offers, was not scrapped and came into the ownership of the South Eastern Railway. It was exhibited at the Stockton and Darlington Railway 50th anniversary in 1875 and at the Newcastle Stephenson Centenary in 1881.

Restoration started in 1892 and for many years *Invicta* was displayed in the Dane John Gardens in Canterbury. Eventually, in 1977, it was fully restored with help from the NRM and returned to Canterbury for the CWR 150th anniversary on May 3, 1980.

It is now to be seen at Poor Priest Hospital, Canterbury, commonly known as the Canterbury Heritage Centre.

Early in SR days, the first private purchase of a main line engine for preservation was when the Railway Correspondence & Travel Society purchased LBSCR 0-4-2 No. 214 *Gladstone,* which was donated to the LNER railway museum at York. Later, the

LSWR T9 4-4-0 No. 30120 arrives at Corfe Castle during the Swanage Railway's LSWR weekend on March 16 2014.

TOP: SR 4-6-0 No. 850 *Lord Nelson* **at Carnforth in September 1980.**

FAR LEFT: Canterbury & Whitstable Railway 0-4-0 *Invicta* **is paraded through the streets of Canterbury on May 5, 1980.** DAVID STAINES

LEFT: LBSCR B1 0-4-2 No. 214 *Gladstone* **at Sheffield Park on the Bluebell Railway in 1982.**

Southern Railway itself laid aside LSWR T3 4-4-0 No. 563 and Brighton 'Terrier' 0-6-0T No. 82 *Boxhill*. The Southern Region of BR followed with SECR D class 4-4-0 No. 737 in 1956 but then private enterprise took the initiative with the Bluebell Railway's purchase of 0-6-0Ts Nos. 31323 and 32636.

In the early 1960s, the British Transport Commission's list of locomotives to be set aside for 'official' preservation was published, and the Southern came out of it quite well; Nos. 30587, 30245, 30120, 30925, 30777 and 30850 being withdrawn and stored soon after publication, to be followed nearer the end of steam by Nos. 33001 and 34051.

The engines selected for 'official' preservation have to be seen in the context of the other Big Four companies. Four Southern engines were already in preservation by 1960, so we already had an LBSCR Stroudley passenger engine, and a Brighton A1 'Terrier', an Adams express 4-4-0 from the LSWR and a Wainwright express 4-4-0 from the SECR.

The Beattie well tank chose itself through the sheer longevity of its use, and the original Bulleid Pacific was an obvious choice, *Winston Churchill* fortunately having avoided the rebuilding process. The Drummond express 4-4-0 of the LSWR No. 120, was one of the most successful 4-4-0s of the period and an interesting comparison with Adams' No. 563, while the M7, also a Drummond design, was representative of the 0-4-4T, also a widely-used type across the country, and of which the M7 was one of the most successful.

For three SR express engines to be selected always seemed a luxury in that No LMS Princess Royal or LNER A3 Pacific was chosen, but the King Arthur 4-6-0 was representative of Urie's designs and the only non-GWR pre-Grouping express design to survive until 1960. The Schools was the ultimate British express 4-4-0 and while the Lord Nelson was another Maunsell express design, it represented a phase in British express steam design which included the original LMS Royal Scots, all of which had by then been rebuilt. Bulleid's Q1 was an unorthodox but successful design and the last and most powerful type of 0-6-0 to be built.

Wainwright had monopolised SECR locomotive design until succeeded by Maunsell and Maunsell was represented by his later designs for the SR. The LSWR saw Adams, Drummond and Urie represented but the Brighton was perhaps unfortunate in being represented only by Stroudley engines, Marsh and Billinton's more notable products all having gone by 1960.

It was too late to save a Brighton Remembrance 4-6-4T, all

> "The British Transport Commission's list of locomotives to be set aside for 'official' preservation was published, and the Southern came out of it quite well"

rebuilt and scrapped, and too late for a Billinton Brighton Atlantic, but with an almost identical Ivatt Great Northern one preserved, it would never have been chosen.

The SR heavy 0-8-4Ts and 4-8-0Ts were too one-off. The SR diesels were not selected for preservation, even the LMS ones were not, and Bulleid's electrics were similarly overlooked. Bulleid's experimental Leader 0-4-4-0T may well have qualified for its novelty value but unfortunately it too was long gone.

Schools class 4-4-0 No. 925 *Cheltenham* **fully restored to operating condition, is seen at the National Railway Museum at York at Railfest 2012.**

CHAPTER 3

Preserved Southern Steam Locomotives

The final total of preserved Southern steam locomotives is impressive; thanks to a combination of public and private enterprise, with many having seen a return to steam.

The Bluebell Railway followed its acquisition of LBSCR A1X 0-6-0T No. 32636 and SECR P Class 0-6-0T No. 31323 with further tank engines, P Class No. 31027 plus the rather larger LSWR 4-4-2T No. 30583 and LBSCR E4 0-6-2T No. 32473. The Kent & East Sussex Railway got in on the act with A1Xs Nos. 32650 and 32670, with the Bluebell getting a further 'Terrier', No. 32655, when the class finally retired.

A1X No. 32640 and Schools 4-4-0 No. 30928 *Stowe* were acquired privately for static preservation and Butlins purchased LSWR B4 0-4-0T No. 30102 and 'Terriers' Nos. 32646, 32678 and 32662 for a similar purpose. Further private purchases, but with a view to active preservation, were SECR 0-6-0s Nos 31065 and 31592, H Class 0-4-4T No. 31263 and LSWR Beattie well tank No. 30585, and purchased for preservation but overseas were A1X No. 32654, LSWR M7 0-4-4T No. 30053 and another Schools, No. 30926 *Repton*. Up to the end of 1966, 21 assorted Southern steam engines entered private preservation.

At the end of Southern Region steam in 1967, preservation societies or individuals secured four USA tanks, Nos. 30064/65/70/72, O2 0-4-4T No. 24 *Calbourne* on the Isle of Wight and two Bulleids, Nos. 34023 *Blackmore Vale* and 35028 *Clan Line*. The future for big steam in the south looked as if it would be at Longmoor, while the South Eastern Steam Centre at Ashford also had big plans.

Surprisingly, four further SR steam engines found their way into preservation after the end of main line steam, having worked in industry: SECR P class 0-6-0Ts Nos. 31178 and 31556, LSWR B4 0-4-0T No. 30096 and LBSCR E1 0-6-0T No. 110. This gave a total of 32 engines privately preserved.

This would have remained the total but for the fact that not all of BR's locomotives sold for scrap were immediately cut up. Dai Woodham, scrap dealer at Barry in South Wales, bought well over 200 steam engines but his workforce was so busy scrapping wagons that very few of the steam engines were ever actually cut up. Of the Southern engines which found their way to Barry, virtually none were scrapped and all those which were in the yard in 1968 were eventually purchased for preservation by 1987.

The flood of purchases from Barry added one N and four U class moguls, six S15 4-6-0s, a Q 0-6-0 and no less than 27 assorted Bulleid Pacifics, more than doubling the total to 71 privately preserved Southern steam engines, plus the 14 National Collection ones. But both Longmoor and Ashford failed, Westerham and the Meon Valley never got off the ground, and it was not until the late 1970s/early 1980s that the Mid-Hants and Swanage railways gave the Bluebell, Isle of Wight and Kent & East Sussex railways some competition, which was really only made possible by the availability of suitable engines from the scrapyard at Barry well after the end of BR steam.

This was not quite the end of the story, as further Southern steam engines are the two imported Jugoslavian USA 0-6-0T 'lookalikes', one running as No. 30075. Another locomotive has been built and steamed in the shape of Lynton & Barnstaple 2ft gauge 2-6-2T No.190 *Lyd*, and a larger new engine is well on the way to completion, Brighton Atlantic No. 32424 *Beachy Head*.

As at 2013, 12 Bulleid Pacifics remain unrestored, eight National Collection engines have remained purely static exhibits throughout, one engine remains in Canada and one S15 is currently nothing more than a kit of parts, having donated most parts to another engine. No less than 65 of the 89 preserved engines have been returned to steam – a remarkable total.

LSWR S15 4-6-0 No. 506 and Bulleid West Country Pacific No. 34105 *Swanage* on shed at Ropley on the Mid-Hants Railway on November 28 1987.

PRESERVED SOUTHERN RAILWAY STEAM LOCOMOTIVES

■ CANTERBURY & WHITSTABLE RAILWAY

			FIRST PRESERVED	CURRENT LOCATION
0-4-0				
Invicta	1830		Canterbury	Canterbury

■ SOUTH EASTERN RAILWAY

O1 0-6-0				
65	1896 (reb 1908)	31065	Ashford	Bluebell

■ SOUTH EASTERN & CHATHAM RAILWAY

C 0-6-0				
592	1900	31592 (DS239)	Ashford	Bluebell
D 4-4-0				
737	1901	31737	Tweedmouth	NRM York
H 0-4-4T				
263	1905	31263	Robertsbridge	Bluebell
P 0-6-0T				
753	1909	31556	KESR	KESR
27	1910	31027	Bluebell	Bluebell
178	1910	31178	Bluebell	Bluebell
323	1910	31323	Bluebell	Bluebell

■ LONDON BRIGHTON & SOUTH COAST RAILWAY

A1 / A1X 0-6-0T				
(70) 3 Bodiam	1872	32670	KESR	KESR
72 Fenchurch	1872	32636	Bluebell	Bluebell
54 Waddon	1875	DS680	Canada	Canada
55 Stepney	1875	32655	Bluebell	Bluebell
62 (Martello)	1875	32662	Heads of Ayr	Bressingham
46 (Newington)	1876	32646	Droxford	Isle of Wight
50 (Whitechapel)	1876	32650	KESR	Spa Valley
40 (Brighton)	1878	32640	Pwllheli	Isle of Wight
78 (Knowle)	1880	32678	Minehead	KESR
82 Boxhill	1880		Nine Elms	NRM York
E1 0-6-0				
110 Burgundy	1877		Hednesford	Isle of Wight
B 0-4-2				
214 Gladstone	1882		York Museum	NRM York
E4 0-6-2T				
473 (Birch Grove)	1898	32473	Bluebell	Bluebell
New-build H2 4-4-2				
Beachy Head		32424	Bluebell	Bluebell

■ LONDON & SOUTH WESTERN RAILWAY

0298 2-4-0WT				
0298	1874	30585	Bishops Stortford	Quainton Road
0314	1875	30587	Fratton	Bodmin
0415 4-4-2T				
488	1885	30583	Bluebell	Bluebell
O2 0-4-4T				
24 Calbourne	1891		Newport	Isle of Wight
T3 4-4-0				
563	1892		Eastleigh	NRM Shildon
B4 0-4-0T				
96 Normandy	1893	30096	Bluebell	Bluebell
102 Granville	1893	30102	Skegness	Bressingham
M7 0-4-4T				
245	1897	30245	Fratton	NRM York
53	1905	30053	USA	Swanage
T9 4-4-0				
120	1899	30120	Eastleigh	Bodmin
S15 4-6-0				
499	1920	30499	MHR	MHR
506	1920	30506	MHR	MHR

■ SOUTHERN RAILWAY

N15 King Arthur 4-6-0				
777 Sir Lamiel	1925	30777	Fratton	GCR
N class 2-6-0				
1874	1925	31874	MHR	MHR
Lord Nelson 4-6-0				
850 Lord Nelson	1925	30850	Fratton	MHR
S15 4-6-0				
825	1927	30825	Brightlingsea	NYMR
828	1927	30828	Eastleigh	MHR
830	1927	30830	Bluebell	NYMR
841	1936	30841	Chappell	NYMR
847	1936	30847	Bluebell	Bluebell

Barry scrapyard in 1975. Nearest the camera is SR U class 2-6-0 No. 31638, later to be preserved on the Bluebell Railway.

			FIRST PRESERVED	CURRENT LOCATION
U class 2-6-0				
1618	1928	31618	New Hythe	Bluebell
1625	1929	31625	MHR	MHR
1638	1931	31638	Bluebell	Bluebell
1806	1928	31806	MHR	MHR
Schools class 4-4-0				
925 Cheltenham	1934	30925	Fratton	MHR
926 Repton	1934	30926	USA	NYMR
928 Stowe	1934	30928	Bealieu Rd	Bluebell
Q class 0-6-0				
541	1939	30541	Ashchurch	Bluebell
Q1 0-6-0				
C1	1942	33001	Stratford	NRM York
USA 0-6-0T				
64	1943	30064	Droxford	Bluebell
65	1943	30065	KESR	Embsay
70	1943	30070	KESR	KESR
72	1943	30072	KWVR	KWVR
	1960	30075	Swanage	Ruddington
		30076	MHR	MHR
West Country 4-6-2				
21C107 Wadebridge	1945	34007	Plym Valley	MHR
21C123 Blackmore Vale	1946	34023	Bluebell	Bluebell
34092 City of Wells	1948		KWVR	KWVR
34105 Swanage	1950		MHR	MHR
Rebuilt West Country 4-6-2				
21C110 Sidmouth	1945	34010	NYMR	Sellindge
21C116 Bodmin	1945	34016	Quainton Road	MHR
21C127 Taw Valley	1946	34027	NYMR	SVR
21C128 Eddystone	1946	34028	Sellindge	Swanage
21C139 Boscastle	1946	34039	GCR	GCR
21C146 Braunton	1946	34046	Preston Park	WSR
34101 Hartland	1950		Sinfin	NYMR
Battle of Britain 4-6-2				
21C151 Winston Churchill	1946	34051	Hellifield	MHR
21C167 Tangmere	1947	34067	MHR	Southall
21C170 Manston	1947	34070	Richborough	Swanage
34072 257 Squadron	1948		Blunsdon	Swanage
34073 249 Squadron	1948		Preston Park	Carnforth
34081 92 Squadron	1948		NVR	NVR
Rebuilt Battle of Britain 4-6-2				
21C153 Sir Keith Park	1947	34053	Hull	SVR
21C158 Sir Frederick Pile	1947	34058	Bitton	MHR
21C159 Sir Archibald Sinclair	1947	34059	Bluebell	Bluebell
Merchant Navy 4-6-2				
35005 Canadian Pacific	1941/59		Carnforth	Eastleigh
35006 Peninsular & Oriental S N Co	1942/57		Glos Warks	Glos Warks
35010 Blue Star	1942/57		North Woolwich	Colne Valley
35011 General Steam Navigation	1944/59		Preston Park	Sellindge
35018 British India Lines	1945/56		MHR	Carnforth
35022 Holland America Line	1948/56		Swanage	Bury
35025 Brocklebank Line	1948/56		GCR	Sellindge
35027 Port Line	1948/57		Blunsdon	Bury
35028 Clan Line	1948/59		Longmoor	Stewarts Lane
35029 Ellerman Lines	1949/59		Market Overton	NRM York

■ LYNTON & BARNSTAPLE RAILWAY

Replica Manning Wardle 2-6-2T				
190 Lyd			Ffestiniog	Ffestiniog

CHAPTER 4

Main Line Steam

With no main line steam for seven years, then only sporadic appearances by Southern engines far removed from home territory, it took a long time to come together but steam on Southern main lines has gone from strength to strength since 1992.

Some remarkable railtours ran on the Southern Region in the 1960s involving preserved steam engines. There were some interlopers such as GNR 0-6-0ST No. 1247, Caledonian Single No. 123, LNER K4 No. 3442 *The Great Marquess*, A3 No. 4472 *Flying Scotsman* and A4 No. 4498 *Sir Nigel Gresley*, but also native power in the shape of LBSCR 'Terrier' 0-6-0T No. 55 *Stepney* and E4 0-6-2T No. 473 *Birch Grove*, and LSWR 4-4-2T No. 488 and T9 'Greyhound' 4-4-0 No. 120.

However, after the end of BR steam in 1967, the electrification of such a significant proportion of the SR system, resulted in virtually no main line steam action on the region throughout the 1970s and much of the 1980s, and main line certificated SR steam engines tended to be seen only north of London.

Merchant Navy Pacific No. 35028 *Clan* Line headed one trip, in non-electrified territory from Eastleigh to Westbury in 1974, and BR Standard 9F 2-10-0 No. 92203 *Black Prince* was seen on the same route but it was not repeated again and it was not until 1986 that steam was finally allowed on the SR again, albeit only on the 42 mile run between Salisbury and Yeovil Junction.

West Country Pacific No. 34027 *Taw Valley's* Folkestone Harbour branch shuttles in September 1991 brought steam back to the Eastern Section after many years and steam ran beyond

Yeovil on occasions, with *Taw Valley* reaching Exeter Central in June 1992 and even St Davids in September 1993.

In the meantime, active Southern steam was in many cases often seen far away from home territory. No. 35028 was based at Hereford, and regularly ran to points even further north. S15 4-6-0 No. 841 had a couple of trips in East Anglia in the late 1970s, before migrating to the North Yorkshire Moors Railway, a line which also played host to West Country Pacific No. 34101 *Hartland* and Schools 4-4-0 No. 30926 *Repton*. The Keighley & Worth Valley Railway had US 0-6-0T No. 72 and more importantly West Country Pacific No. 34092 *City of Wells*, which did make one memorable visit to the Southern Region from Yorkshire, but not until 1988. The National Collection's two SR express 4-6-0s No. 777 *Sir Lamiel* and No. 850 *Lord Nelson* were very much northern engines in the 1980s after restoration.

The real main line breakthrough on the Southern did not come until 1992 when Severn Valley-based No. 34027 *Taw Valley* ran from Waterloo to Bournemouth, but after dark. With no serious trespass problems being encountered, steam was eventually permitted in daylight on electrified routes from 1994 and the Mid-Hants Railway unexpectedly took the plunge into main line operation in 1998 with its Daylight Railtours

Soon after departing from Victoria, N15 King Arthur class 4-6-0 No. 30777 *Sir Lamiel* passes Wandsworth Road on November 6, 1994.

On a trip noted for some spirited running, West Country Pacific No. 34092 *City of Wells* passes Barford St Martin with a 'Blackmore Vale Express' on July 24, 1988.

programme using its own locomotives and stock – the Green Train, and not only did the Mid-Hants turn out West Country No. 34016 *Bodmin* but moguls Nos. 31806 and 31625 as well, followed by Merchant Navy No. 35005 *Canadian Pacific*.

Privatisation of the main line network really opened the floodgates for main line steam on the Southern, and steam is almost an everyday sight on the main line in the 21st century.

Clan Line remained the spiritual leader of the Southern steam revival and spearheaded the use of air brakes on preserved main line steam in the UK in 1994, leading of course to its regular use on the Venice Simplon-Orient Express Pullmans, recreating the sight of the SR's premier Pullman steam workings.

However, although Daylight Railtours proved very successful for seven years and raised the profile of the MHR through the south and west of England, it became increasingly difficult to organise the tours, particularly getting the train in and out of Alton at reasonable times, and the operation ceased at the end of 2004 with the coaches being sold, although still based on the railway and hired out for the Steam Dreams' expanding 'Cathedrals Express' programme for some years.

Steam Dreams was the brainchild of enthusiast Marcus Robertson whose mother wrote the TV series The Wombles. It differed from Daylight Railtours in being more orientated to the general public than the enthusiast, but has nevertheless always attracted a substantial enthusiast following. In 2000 the first 'Cathedrals Express' left London for Canterbury and the operation has gone from strength to strength, though it by no means has a monopoly of SR main line steam working.

The reconnection of the Bluebell Railway to the main line network in 2013, means that all three major lines now have a main line connection and the potential for further expansion of steam operations on heritage lines and the main lines in the future is almost endless.

While based at Hereford, Merchant Navy Pacific No. 35028 *Clan Line* passes Marshbrook on the Welsh Marches route on September 29, 1984.

West Country Pacific No. 34027 *Taw Valley* at Clapham Junction on September 11, 1992, prior to working the ground-breaking first steam departure from Waterloo since 1967.

South Eastern & Chatham Railway

With some of Britain's most elegant steam locomotives, the SECR, as a result of its two constituent companies, was nevertheless noted for the poor quality of its train services, yet it made a significant contribution to the development of Britain's railways.

O ne of the three major constituents of the Southern Railway in 1923, the South Eastern and Chatham Railway was not an actual company but a joint management committee representing two former rival railways, the South Eastern Railway and the London, Chatham and Dover Railway. From January 1, 1899, the SECR operated between London and south-east England, with a monopoly of railway services in Kent, and to the main Channel ports for ferries to France and Belgium.

The companies had competed bitterly and both were notorious for the poor quality of their track and services and the decrepit nature of their stock. The merger had been almost inevitable.

The SECR's first locomotive carriage and wagon superintendent was Harry Smith Wainwright, who had held the position on the SER from 1896, and was known for several distinctive designs of locomotive which were built at Ashford works, many of which survived in service until the 1960s, although they tended to be more elegant than powerful.

The first Wainwright designs for the SECR began to appear in 1900; the 109-strong C class 0-6-0, followed by the 51 D class 4-4-0s. In almost all cases, the actual design work was supervised by Robert Surtees, formerly chief draughtsman on the LCDR, following Wainwright's basic specification, with the latter more involved in the final finish and livery.

Wainwright retired on November 30, 1913, and died on September 19, 1925. He was succeeded by Richard Edward Lloyd Maunsell, who was given the title of chief mechanical engineer.

Maunsell was born on May 26, 1868, at Raheny, Co Dublin, and after graduating from Trinity College, Dublin, he began an apprenticeship at the Inchicore works of the Great Southern and Western Railway under HA Ivatt in 1886, completing his training at Horwich Works on the Lancashire and Yorkshire Railway, then working for two years in India. He returned to Britain in 1896 to become works manager at Inchicore on the Great Southern & western Railway in Ireland, becoming locomotive superintendent in 1911 but quickly moving on to the SECR in 1913.

The First World War prevented Maunsell from producing many new designs for the SECR although he rebuilt many Wainwright engines, making them more powerful but less elegant. He introduced the N class 2-6-0 and K class (River) 2-6-4T though.

The tanks were later converted to 2-6-0 tender locomotives and these N class and U class moguls became standard mixed traffic power across the Southern Railway following Nationalisation.

In Wainwright's day, SECR locomotives and rolling stock were noted for their superb standards of appearance and presentation, with his locomotive livery in particular being considered among the most elaborate and decorative of any British railway. After Maunsell's takeover just before the First World War, the livery was simplified though and eventually replaced with unlined grey/green. Plain brown also replaced lined crimson lake on coaching stock, apart from the Pullman cars. The SECR had electrification plans but these came to nothing although the suburban routes became a priority in SR days.

The London Chatham & Dover Railway coat-of-arms on the bridge over the Thames at Cannon Street.

D Class 4-4-0 No. 737

The SECR D class 4-4-0 was designed by locomotive superintendent Harry Wainwright who was responsible for the overall look of the engine, but the detail design was the work of chief draughtsman Robert Surtees. A particularly graceful design, the D class was nevertheless powerful. The first 20 engines were built at Ashford works and by Sharp Stewart and Co in Glasgow. The first in service, in 1901, was a Sharp Stewart engine and by 1907, 51 were in traffic, built either at Ashford or by outside contractors.

The D class started work on the Kent coast and Hastings services out of London, but as soon as 1913, Wainwright's successor Richard Maunsell started rebuilding 21 of the class with Belpaire fireboxes to produce the more powerful D1 class, which were needed to cope with increasing loads on the Kent coast line. The new design had little of the elegance of the original though.

By the 1930s, in SR days, the largest allocation of the remaining D class engines was at Gillingham but they had by now been demoted to secondary duties, and in 1939 some were put in store. In 1941 others were transferred to Nine Elms, while a handful were based at Redhill to work on the Reading-Tonbridge cross-country line.

Twenty-eight of the Wainwright 4-4-0s made it into BR ownership in 1948, and they became concentrated at Guildford, the last of the class, No. 31075, being withdrawn from there in 1956.

No. 31737 was preserved by British Railways and found itself in the unlikely setting of the North Eastern Railway's Tweedmouth roundhouse for a while until it was restored to SECR livery at Ashford works as No. 737 and put on display ready for the opening of the British Transport Museum at Clapham, where it had arrived on June 26, 1960.

In 1974, it was moved by rail to the National Railway Museum at York where it has remained on show, but it has never steamed in preservation.

The elegant Wainwright D class 4-4-0 No. 737 at the National Railway Museum at York.

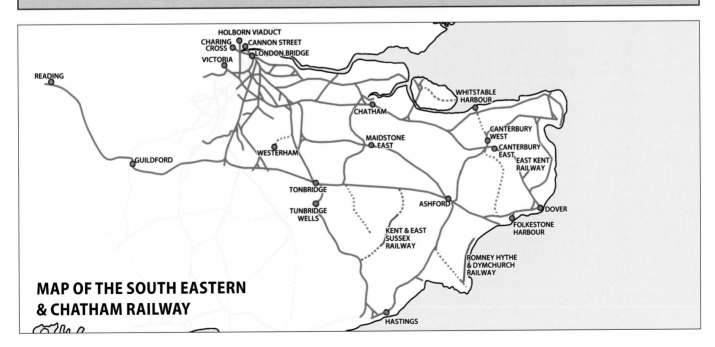

MAP OF THE SOUTH EASTERN & CHATHAM RAILWAY

On the line where it ran during the 1950s and where it hauled demolition trains, No. 65 runs round its train at Bodiam on the Kent & East Sussex Railway on May 3, 2009.
PHIL BARNES

SECR O1 0-6-0 No. 65 on display in the locomotive shed at Sheffield Park on the Bluebell Railway

O1 0-6-0 No. 65

The South Eastern Railway O class 0-6-0, of which some were rebuilt to become the O1, was the main freight engine of the SER, and later the SECR for a number of years, until displaced by Wainwright's larger C class. This relegated the class to working branch lines in Kent, on both passenger and freight work. They worked notably on the former Colonel Stephens Kent & East Sussex and East Kent railways, operating coal trains from the Kent coalfields to London, as well as shunting work.

All 59 O1s made it to Southern Railway stock, but the majority were withdrawn before the Second World War, and those that remained were slowly withdrawn from Nationalisation onwards, all being condemned by 1962.

No. 65 was built in 1896, and is the only surviving former SER locomotive, although it was rebuilt in 1908, also at Ashford, and is

similar to the SECR C class. Its original designer, Stirling, had kept the axle weight very low because of the SER's poor track and this was perpetuated by Wainwright, resulting in engines literally able to go anywhere, which contributed to No. 65's longevity.

Originally an Ashford engine, in Southern Railway days, No. 1065 was employed on banking duties at Folkestone Harbour. In BR days, No. 31065 was back at Ashford and by 1958, was one of eight survivors. A moment of glory came when, doubleheaded with C class No. 31592, it worked the last train on the Hawkhurst branch, but it was condemned 13 days later on June 24, 1961, after 1,388,000 miles of service over 66 years.

Surprisingly it was still in store at Bricklayers' Arms shed in early 1963, and was purchased by Esmond Lewis-Evans for the scrap value of £850. The connecting rods had already been cut,

**SECR O1 0-6-0 No. 65 and
C class No. 592 join forces
for an early morning
goods train of mainly
pre-Grouping wagons on
the Bluebell Railway.**
JON BOWERS

but this was rectified. It was moved to the Ashford Steam Centre, established by Mr Lewis-Evans and others, based on part of the former Ashford Works. There, the engine worked during open days along with C class No. 592 and H class 0-4-4T No. 263, all three later to become Bluebell Railway residents.

When the centre was closed, No. 65 faced an uncertain future. While most engines moved to established centres or railways, the O1, needing a general overhaul, ended up on a private site in Kent in 1983, where it was split into frames, boiler, and tender, and items such as cab fittings etc. removed.

Although limited progress was made, no serious attempt at restoration was made for 20 years, as it was beyond the owner's resources. In 1996, Mr Lewis-Evans was approached by the Bluebell Railway to take his engine to Sheffield Park, with a view

to early restoration. Moved on June 21, 1997, the major overhaul was immediately commenced.

The work was completed remarkably quickly and the engine was returned to traffic for the centenary of the amalgamation of the SER and LCDR into the SECR by 1999, finished in ornate SECR goods livery.

It performed regularly at the Bluebell Railway and in May 2009, made a historic return to the K&ESR, having been a regular on the line during the 1950s, including working some of the demolition trains.

The engine's boiler certificate expired in July 2009, but is not thought to require much work to restore it, and there may soon be the potential for five ex-SECR engines to be operational together for the first time since the 1960s.

C class 0-6-0 No. 592 at Sheffield Park on May 11, 1983.

C class 0-6-0 No. 592

After the amalgamation of the SER and the LCDR in 1899, Harry Wainwright introduced some order into the variety of locomotive designs from the two constituent companies.

The C class 0-6-0 was his standard goods design to supersede earlier types, and 109 of them were built between 1900 and 1908. They lasted well, with 106 being inherited by BR in 1948, and 60 remaining in service in 1960. A useful feature of the design was the steam powered reverser still used on goods and shunting engines built by the SECR and the SR for more than 40 years afterwards.

No. 592 is seen at the foot of Freshfield bank on the Bluebell Railway.

The last three of the class survived in departmental service at Ashford works, and the C Class Preservation Society was formed in 1962 to purchase one for preservation. In December 1966, the society was able to buy DS237, the former No. 31592. The South Eastern Steam Centre was set up in the old running shed at Ashford, and this became the 0-6-0's home. When the venture failed, No. 592 was moved to the Bluebell Railway on August 16, 1970, where it finally entered service in May 1975 after repairs to its boiler and a badly damaged axle journal.

A further overhaul was completed in 1994 and it returned to service with a spare tender, obtained from Folkestone, where it had been used as a mobile water tank. A spare boiler, formerly a stationary boiler at Ashford, was overhauled in 2006/7, as the firebox of the existing boiler was beyond repair. It returned to service on October 8, 2007, but is likely to require a new cylinder block shortly. In 2014, the engine remains in regular use.

H class 0-4-4T No. 263

The two constituents of the SECR had both relied on 0-4-4Ts for London suburban, and semi-fast train services; the SER Q class of 1887, and the LCDR R class of 1891. The R was the better design, and was continued in production by Harry Wainwright after amalgamation in 1899. However, as traffic continued to increase there was a need for a new more powerful 0-4-4T design to take over from the Q class and so Wainwright came up with an updated version of the R class.

Seven locomotives were built at Ashford in 1904 and were found to be successful; a total of 64 being built by 1909, with two more in 1915. The H class boiler design was found to be so successful that it was later used as a standard replacement boiler on various other SER, LCDR and SECR classes.

64 of the class entered British Railways stock in 1948, by which time they were largely displaced from their original duties by electrification but found work elsewhere on the Eastern and Central sections and even the Western Section. 45 were equipped for push-pull working between 1949 and 1960, and were increasingly used on motor-trains on rural branches, but most were withdrawn by 1962, except for a few working the non-electrified lines between Tunbridge Wells and Three Bridges.

The final member of the class, No. 31263 (SECR No. 263), was withdrawn from Three Bridges on January 4, 1964, but remained in store at the shed until the following November, when it was purchased by the H-Class Trust and was preserved initially at Robertsbridge close to the Kent & East Sussex Railway. It moved to the South Eastern Steam Centre at Ashford on February 2, 1969, where it was occasionally steamed but on January 25, 1976, moved to the Bluebell Railway, where it saw more regular use. In 2008 ownership was transferred to the Bluebell Railway Trust, prior to an overhaul which was completed by July 2012.

H class 0-4-4T No. 263 departs from Sheffield Park on the Bluebell Railway on June 21, 1997.

No. 263 in steam at an open day at the South Eastern Steam Centre at Ashford on June 13, 1971. DON BENN

P class 0-6-0T

The P Class 0-6-0Ts were introduced in 1909 by the South Eastern and Chatham Railway to a design by Harry Wainwright, mainly for light branch passenger services, especially between Nunhead Junction and Greenwich Park, Otford and Sevenoaks, and between Reading and Ash. The engines were found to be too small for such work though, being little better than the steam railmotors they were meant to replace and they were soon distributed over the system for light shunting duties and as shed pilots, which they were ideal for, since they possessed the excellent SECR steam reverser.

Similar in size to the LBSCR A1 'Terrier' 0-6-0Ts, they were not as successful in service but nevertheless they all lasted into BR days and no less than four of the eight built still survive today.

In Southern livery, No. 1556 climbs Tenterden bank with a goods train on October 25, 1993.
PHIL BARNES

ABOVE: P class 0-6-0T 1556 at the CF de Baie de la Somme on one of its visits to the French heritage line on April 28, 1996.

RIGHT: Fully restored to SECR livery, P class 0-6-0T No. 753 is seen at Tenterden on the Kent & East Sussex Railway. GERALD SIVIOUR

P Class 0-6-0T No. 753

No. 753 was the first of the P class 0-6-0Ts built at Ashford works entering traffic on February 18, 1909 on the Sevenoaks to Otford line.

From April 1915 to October 1916, No. 753, along with No. 27, now on the Bluebell Railway, was shipped across the Channel for war service at Boulogne, painted olive green and numbered as ROD No. 5753. On its return, No. 753 worked between Swanley and Gravesend West for a while but was Redhill carriage pilot by 1923. Successive renumberings saw it as No. 1556 in SR days after 1931. Like many class members it moved to Dover and Folkestone to work the harbours, but during 1936 and again in 1938 it was hired to the KESR which was temporarily short of motive power, and a further period of hire occurred in 1947. Under BR ownership as No. 31556, it was at Brighton, working as shed pilot and at Shoreham harbour, until withdrawal in April 1961, as the longest serving P class.

But No. 31556 was sold to James Hodson & Sons' flour mill at Robertsbridge, in June 1961, where it was named *Pride of Sussex*. For nearly 10 years it worked around the mill and on the private siding leading to the station yard which was originally part of the KESR. On closure of the siding it was a natural choice for purchase by the preserved KESR in 1970.

It was steamed a few times on the railway, nominally being No. 11 but was dismantled in 1973 for major boiler repairs and mechanical overhaul. It spent 10 years in a stripped down state but during 1984-86 steady progress was made and the locomotive returned to service in SR black livery as No. 1556. On two occasions it has revisited France, to take part in the KESR's twinning with the CF de Baie de la Somme. It was overhauled again after 1997 and returned to traffic in 2001 in the full glory of its original SECR livery.

P class 0-6-0T No. 27

Before the First World War, SECR P class 0-6-0T No. 27 was allocated to Reading shed but during the war, together with No. 753 (now preserved on the KESR), was shipped across the Channel for war service at Boulogne, carrying the ROD number 5027.

P class 0-6-0T No. 27 at Sheffield Park on the Bluebell Railway.
JEFF COLLEDGE

Allocated to Dover for much of its BR service, as No. 31027, the P class was the third engine purchased by the Bluebell Railway, arriving on June 18, 1961 and entering service immediately. Reverting to its original number 27, for two years it carried the name *Primrose*, but in 1963 it was repainted into full SECR passenger livery, and, with its sister No. 323, was a mainstay of the Bluebell's operational fleet for much of the 1960s. It was withdrawn in November 1974 requiring overhaul. Like many older engines purchased from BR in the early 1960s, it arrived in steamable condition and worked for many years but once withdrawn it was a considerable time since its last BR overhaul and extensive work would be required to return it to service.

No. 27 was dismantled in 1978 but the restoration stalled and did not recommence for nearly 30 years. The work on the locomotive is now being carried out by volunteers, supported by the fundraising efforts of the 'Fenchurch Fund'. Major work is required on the boiler and frames, as well as some significant mechanical renewal and replacement of platework, including the tanks.

P class 0-6-0T No. 1178

No. 178 was built at Ashford works in 1910 and its first allocation was to Ash, a sub-shed of Reading, which had both GWR and SECR stations and sheds. Its main duties were working the push-pull service to Aldershot, but the success of these services resulted in heavier trains and the P class was replaced by more powerful locomotives so No.178 was transferred to the South London area to work the Beckenham Junction to Norwood Junction service. In the period immediately before the outbreak of the First World War, it was based at Longhedge and regularly worked on Victoria/St.Pauls shuttles and to Greenwich Park from Nunhead and Victoria.

Soon after the outbreak of war, No 178 was allocated to Margate for local passenger trains, then to Redhill for carriage shunting duties and on to Kidbrooke in South London. January 1917 saw it allocated to Bricklayers Arms shed, followed by a spell at Orpington working the Swanley to Otford shuttles, then Tonbridge, from where No. 178 spent several years operating over the Westerham branch, along with sister engine No. 323.

It was renumbered 1178 at the Grouping, but in 1926 all the P class was withdrawn from passenger duties and it was transferred to Folkestone and then to Dover and operated in that area for many years mainly on light shunting duties around the docks. 1943 though saw a temporary transfer to Brighton.

During 1953, after Nationalisation, the P underwent trials against an LSWR B4 0-4-0T in which the SECR engine compared unfavourably, so No. 31178 was reduced to a standby status for dock shunting at Dover, but continued to shunt elsewhere for several years, with a spell on loan to the Ridham Dock exchange siding of Bowaters paper mills in 1953, and Chislet colliery in the Kent coalfield in 1955.

A transfer back to Bricklayers Arms later in 1955 ended with replacement by a diesel shunter and No. 31178 returned on loan to Bowaters in 1956, but after a visit to Ashford for repairs, its final allocation was to Stewarts Lane, Battersea, to shunt the milk depot.

No 31178 was then withdrawn but sold to Bowaters, returning to familiar territory at Ridham Dock. Repainted in a version of SECR livery and named *Pioneer II*, it worked there until 1969, when it was

withdrawn with serious cylinder damage. However, the Bluebell Railway was given a late opportunity to acquire its third P class and *Pioneer II* moved to Sheffield Park in October 1969.

Although more use as a source of spare parts, a group of *Port Line* shareholders purchased the locomotive in 1989 for eventual restoration, but the team was busy with other major projects, and still little progress was made.

The Bluebell has four P class boilers, and while one was in use on No. 323, the second-best one was provided for No. 178, being the one which was carried by No. 323 when it arrived on the line in 1960.

Eventually it was agreed that ownership should revert to the Bluebell Railway in mid 2006, with funding made available by the Bluebell Railway Trust. Work resumed on the engine in 2007, with labour being provided by the Loco Workshop Working Group. The locomotive returned to service at the end of February 2010, and on Saturday, May 1, 2010, No.178 was officially launched into traffic. It is now in full SECR livery, following a brief appearance in Bowaters' livery.

On February 27, 2010, the Bluebell Railway operated trains only between Sheffield Park and Horsted Keynes, to its 1963 timetable, calling at Freshfield, Holywell and Bluebell Halts. Briefly carrying its Bowaters livery as *Pioneer II*, P class No. 178 heads the line's Metropolitan coaching set.
TERRY BLACKMAN

Bluebell on shed at Sheffield Park. ROBIN JONES

P class 0-6-0T 323 *Bluebell*

The Bluebell Railway's first locomotive was an appropriate Brighton 'Terrier' 0-6-0T in May 1960 but a second engine was required before it would be able to start operating trains. No other 'Terriers' were available but BR offered a similar sized SECR P class, No. 31323. The railway bought it with some reluctance, but after arriving on June 2, 1960, the SECR engine proved the equal of the 'Terrier', and another P, No. 27 was purchased a year later.

No. 31323 entered service immediately and soon carried ornate blue livery as No. 323, named *Bluebell*. From 1980 to 1984, *Bluebell* was hired to the East Somerset Railway.

Having last been overhauled in 1989 to operate the northern extension shuttles, *Bluebell* continued to give good service on a variety of duties until being withdrawn for overhaul in February 2000.

Although in 2009, as one of the two original engines which

were used to reopen the line in 1960, it was decided as a priority to get it running for the railway's 50th anniversary celebrations the following year, this proved impossible as there was a need for additional boiler repairs. However, after this additional work, No. 323 returned to service just in time to put in an appearance at the branch line weekend in March 2011.

P class 0-6-0T No. 323 *Bluebell* rounds the curve at the top of Freshfield bank on the Bluebell Railway on May 13, 1979.

CHAPTER 6

London Brighton & South Coast Railway

Serving the south coast between Hastings and Portsmouth, the 'Brighton' had some distinctive locomotive classes but although many survived into the 1950s, they were early withdrawals by BR and comparatively few classes are now represented in preservation.

The London, Brighton and South Coast Railway was formed by a merger of five former railway companies and came into existence in 1846. Two of the constituents were the London and Croydon Railway, one of the earliest railways in the south, opened in 1839, also the London and Brighton Railway. This opened from London Bridge to Brighton in 1841.

The LBSCR's triangular territory lay between the South Eastern & Chatham Railway and the London & South Western Railway, with London at the top, virtually the whole coastline of Sussex at the bottom, plus a sizeable section of Surrey.

The LBSCR's services formed the most direct routes from London to the coastal resorts of Brighton, Eastbourne, Worthing, Bognor Regis and Littlehampton. In addition it served Shoreham-by-Sea and Newhaven ports. The London area was a complicated network of suburban and outer-suburban lines, radiating from Victoria and London Bridge.

During its beginnings, the LBSCR had around 170 route miles in existence or in construction.

The LBSCR was a pioneer in its use of electricfication due to the nature of the line's traffic. It had a sizeable number of short commuter journeys.

Third and fourth rail DC systems had been chosen for the underground tube railways and other lines. However, the LBSCR decided on a 6600v overhead system, more appropriate for future main line electrification. The South London Line was the first section to undergo electrification, this linking London Bridge with Victoria via Denmark Hill.

The railway decided to electrify all remaining London suburban lines in 1913, and although the Second World War delayed this, by 1921 most of the inner London suburban lines were electrified, and plans were being made to extend the wires to Worthing, Eastbourne, Newhaven and Seaford.

A1X 0-6-0Ts No. 55 Stepney and No. 32636 storm up Freshfield bank on the Bluebell Railway on January 29, 1989.

LBSCR B class 0-4-2 No. 214 *Gladstone*

The B class was the last express passenger design William Stroudley created, it was a bigger and revised version of the Richmond class created in 1878. Brighton works produced 36 of the class between 1882 and 1891, and were used on the heaviest London to Brighton expresses, all named after politicians, men associated with the railway, or places served by the railway.

DE Marsh later designated the class B1, though this was gradually replaced by Billinton B4 class 4-4-0s and were transferred to secondary duties. Withdrawal began in April 1910, but 26 passed to the SR in 1923, the last survivor, No. 172, being withdrawn in 1933.

In 1927, the Stephenson Locomotive Society had made representation to the Southern Railway to preserve the old No. 214, now No. 618 *Gladstone*. This was the first main line steam engine to be purchased privately for preservation for £150. It was restored closely to Stroudley condition, with the addition of various period fittings. The intention was originally to place it on permanent exhibition in the Science Museum in London, but this was impracticable at the time and it ended up at the LNER's railway museum at York on May 31, 1927, where it remained until transferred to the new National Railway Museum in 1975.

Gladstone has never steamed in preservation.

ABOVE: LBSCR B class 0-4-2 No. 214 *Gladstone* on display at the National Railway Museum at York.

LEFT: The original receipt for *Gladstone* for the sum of £150.

However, when the LBSCR became part of the Southern Railway in 1923, the neighbouring London & South Western Railway had far more electrified mileage, but on the third-rail DC system. Inevitably the SR standardised on the LSWR system.

The LBSCR inherited 51 steam locomotives from its predecessors and put another 1055 locomotives into service. Of these 62 passed to the Southern Railway in 1923.

Locomotive superintendent from 1847 to 1869, John Chester Craven, designed different locomotives for each type of traffic, resulting in 72 different classes. Successor William Stroudley was then left the task of resolving this situation.

One of the 19th century's best-known locomotive engineers, Stroudley introduced many very successful and long-lived designs, notably the A1 'Terrier' 0-6-0T and the B1 class 0-4-2 express passenger locomotives. None had more than six wheels though, because of the line's small turntables.

Following this R J Billington, Stroudly's successor, continued the process of standardisation and finally introduced big 4-4-0s and 0-6-2 tank engines, these with radial rear axles.

After 1904, DE Marsh continued the process of building larger locomotives with two classes of express locomotives for passenger service in 4-4-2s and four classes of 4-4-2Ts and two classes of 4-6-2s. However, between 1905 and 1912 the railway suffered an increasingly serious motive power shortage due to the inability of the Brighton works to keep pace with the volume of repairs and new construction required, leading to Marsh's sickness and retirement.

The last CME of the railway was L Billinton, designer of K class 2-6-0 of 1913, and the L class 4-6-4 Ts of 1914, but his career was cut short by the War and the Grouping of 1923.

LB&SCR designs had little impact on the locomotive policy of the Southern Railway after 1923 because they were built to a generous loading gauge, fitted with Westinghouse air brakes. This however led to a higher proportion of the LBSCR's locomotives that had been inherited by the Southern Railway being handed over to British Railways in 1948, than that of the other two major SR constituent companies, although many were extensively rebuilt. Brighton engines fared badly under BR and few survived into the 1960s.

From 1900, the LBSCR's two-digit numbers were prefixed with a '6' and their names were replaced with the inscription 'LBSC' on their side tanks (for example, No. 55 *Stepney* became No. 655). This was fairly standard LBSCR practice; as engines got old, they were given higher numbers so that newer engines could have lower numbers.

A1X 0-6-0T No. 55 *Stepney* and No. 32636 approach Horsted Keynes on the Bluebell Railway on January 29, 1989.

A1 and A1X class 0-6-0T 'Terriers'

The statistics relating to preserved SR steam engines are interesting; Three main pre-Grouping companies made up the Southern Railway in 1923; of these eight SECR engines are preserved and 10 LSWR ones but no less than 14 LBSCR ones, 10 of which are 'Terriers'.

Originally known as the A class, these small tank engines were designed by William Stroudley in 1870 to work commuter trains on the busy lines in south London, including the East London Railway through the Thames Tunnel designed by Marc Isambard Brunel. Six locomotives were built for these services during 1872, and with proven power and acceleration with heavy trains between the closely-spaced stations, immediately proved successful. A further 44 were built by September 1880.

The locomotives were originally numbered 35-84, and most carried names of London boroughs which were served by LBSCR suburban trains, with exceptions such as *Boxhill*. They were finished in the livery known as Stroudley's 'improved engine green', said to be a result of colour-blindness, from which Stroudley supposedly suffered.

23 of the class, which quickly acquired the nickname 'Terriers', were withdrawn around the turn of the century, with the survivors being redesignated A1s, but the majority of these were sold for further service rather than scrapped. 'Terriers' found their way to the the LSWR, the SECR, the Newhaven Harbour Company, the Isle of Wight Central Railway, and the Kent and East Sussex Railway. The LBSCR survivors got a new lease of life, being found to be ideal for push-pull working, then being adopted on many lightly-used branch line services

Between 1911 and 1913, 12 of the survivors were reboilered by Stroudley's successor, DE Marsh, with another four later, then becoming the A1X class with an increased weight and other modifications, also being repainted during this time in Marsh umber livery and losing their names.

Some 15 remained in LBSCR stock at the formation of the Southern Railway in 1923, but this was of course increased to 24 by those which had previously been sold to other SR constituents. Further 'Terriers' were withdrawn over the next few years, two being sold to the independent Weston, Clevedon and Portishead Railway, and among the engines withdrawn was the now-famous No. 55 *Stepney*.

The class lasted longer than most classes of pre-Grouping tank engine on the Southern Railway, primarily due to the fact that the SR inherited many very lightly-laid lines, such as the Hayling Island branch, KESR and Isle of Wight lines.

At Nationalisation in 1948, one A1 and 14 A1Xs entered BR stock, all but one on the Southern Region, the exception being one of the WC&P ones which came under the Western Region. By the early 1960s, the class was concentrated on the KESR and Hayling Island branch, and the former closed in 1961.

The Hayling Island branch may have survived longer but the Southern Region considered the bridge over Langstone Harbour as being beyond economic repair. It closed on November 3, 1963, with Nos. 32650, 32662 and 32670 working on the last day, and a special 'topped and tailed' by Nos. 32636 and 32670 the following day. The last five 'Terriers', some over 90 years old, were withdrawn.

A1X 0-6-0T No. 72 *Fenchurch* and No. 55 *Stepney* at Sheffield Park on the Bluebell Railway on September 12, 1983.

A1X 0-6-0T No. 72 *Fenchurch*

The first of the class to enter service, No. 72 was one of the class which became surplus to the requirements of the LBSCR and was sold as long ago as 1898 to the Newhaven Harbour Company, but still found itself taken into Southern Railway stock in 1927.

The oldest surviving 'Terrier', and at the time, the oldest locomotive working on BR, No. 32636, together with No. 32670 hauled the Hayling Island farewell railtour on November 3, 1963. It was one of the last to be withdrawn and was purchased by the Bluebell Railway, arriving on the line on May 13, 1964, under its own steam from Eastleigh via Brighton. After considerable use, the locomotive was retired for overhaul in 1970, but returned to traffic in 1972 for its centenary. However, it was withdrawn in 1975 after an appearance at the Rail 150 cavalcade at Shildon marking the anniversary of opening of the Stockton & Darlington Railway, then with a new firebox re-entered service in 1980, running until 1988.

At its next overhaul, the need to replace one pair of the original wrought iron wheels because of cracks in a wheel-hub meant the locomotive was not returned to traffic until 2001. Although carrying an A1X boiler, the smokebox was rebuilt during that overhaul and it now looks very similar to its original A1 form.

A1X 0-6-0T No. 3 *Bodiam*

No. 70 *Poplar* is the second oldest of the surviving 'Terriers', having been built at Brighton works in December 1872. The Bluebell Railway's No. 72 *Fenchurch* also came from this batch, entering service just before *Poplar*. The name *Poplar*, reflects that the class was mainly intended for work on the East London line.

After nearly 30 years service for the LBSCR, the engine was sold to Col. Stephens for use on the newly opened Rother Valley Railway, more familiar as the Kent & East Sussex Railway from 1904, where it worked until closure to passengers in 1954. It was never owned by the Southern Railway and carried the number 3 until BR renumbered it 32670 in 1948.

No. 32670 survived the closure of the KESR to passenger services, and then saw much service on the Hayling Island branch, but closure of the branch in 1963 resulted in its withdrawal.

No. 32670 was initially purchased by the Wheels brothers of Brighton in 1964, arriving on the KESR on April 11, 1964, and usually running as KESR No. 3 *Bodiam*, hauling the first train on the restored heritage line on February 3, 1974. Following withdrawal in 1977, it was overhauled and returned to service as No. 32670 on August 1, 1984. However, it later found itself out of use for a decade before the KESR and The Terrier Trust bought it and agreed a restoration plan. It returned to traffic in May 2006 in original Rother Valley Railway livery of Oxford blue, then in April 2011 was again repainted BR black as No. 32670, to feature at the Last Train Commemoration that took place on June 11 that year.

In Oxford blue livery, Kent & East Sussex Railway A1X 0-6-0T No. 3 *Bodiam*. PHIL BARNES

LBSCR 'Terrier' 0-6-0T No. 54 *Waddon*, coupled to the Canadian museum's replica 2-2-2 *John Molson* (based on an 1849-built locomotive supplied by Kinmonds, Hutton and Steel of Dundee for the Champlain & St Lawrence Railway, shows off its retouched livery. PETER CUNNINGHAM

A1 0-6-0T No. 54 *Waddon*

No. 54 *Waddon* was not rebuilt as an A1X, having been fitted with an SECR boiler after being sold to that railway for £670, where it became its No. 75, still entering into SR stock at the Grouping.

In 1932, No. 751, still in SECR livery, emerged from Brighton works as departmental No. 680S, fitted with an A1X boiler, but retaining the shorter A1-type smokebox and spent most of its time at Lancing carriage works.

It became BR departmental DS680 and not withdrawn until May 1962, after which it was almost immediately donated by BR to the Canada Railway Historical Association. Despite this, it occasionally continued to be used at Lancing until December when it went to Brighton where it was sometimes used as shed pilot before returning to Lancing. It steamed to Eastleigh on February 23, 1963 for restoration to original condition and was shipped to Canada on August 23, 1963. After a number of years stored in the open, British ex-pats living in Canada formed a group to work on the locomotive and restore it to pristine condition, along with LNER A4 Pacific, No. 60010 *Dominion of Canada*, which is also based at the museum in Montreal.

A1X 0-6-0T No. 55 *Stepney*

No. 32655, together with No. 32678, was involved in the last day of passenger services on the Kent & East Sussex Railway on January 2, 1954. It had narrowly escaped withdrawal on 1905, yet survived to receive a new boiler in 1959.

No. 32655 was the first engine to arrive at the Bluebell Railway, the first standard gauge preserved line in Britain, arriving on May 17, 1960, becoming the first BR steam engine to be purchased for use on a preserved steam railway. It arrived at Horsted Keynes under its own steam from Brighton hauling the two carriages the society had purchased and went on to haul the reopening train in August of that year.

Reverting to its original identity as No. 55 *Stepney*, it worked two main line railtours on the Southern Region. The first ran on October 21, 1962 and saw No. 55 doublehead with LSWR Adams 4-4-2T No. 488 on the Haywards Heath to Horsted Keynes and return section of a tour from London Victoria to the Bluebell Railway. The second one ran from Brighton to Horsted Keynes on October 27, 1963 for members of the Bluebell Railway Preservation Society, with the locomotive doubleheading with another former LBSCR locomotive, E4 0-6-2T No. 473 *Birch Grove*. It marked the closure of the line from Haywards Heath to Horsted Keynes.

A1X 0-6-0T No. 55 *Stepney* pilots E4 0-6-2T No. 473 on Freshfield bank on October 26, 2003, 50 years after the two locomotives doubleheaded the farewell railtour from Brighton to Horsted Keynes.

***Stepney* at Railfest at the National Railway Museum at York, May 2012.**

A1X 0-6-0Ts No. 662 *Martello*, No. 3 *Bodiam* and No. 32678 at the KESR Last Trains Gone gala of May 3, 2009. PHIL BARNES

A1X 0-6-0T No. 32662 on display at Butlins Heads of Ayr holiday camp with LMS Pacific No. 6233 *Duchess of Sutherland*.
COLOUR-RAIL.COM

BELOW: A1X 0-6-0T No. 10 departs from Tenterden on July 29, 1984.

A1X 0-6-0T No. 662 *Martello*

No. 62 *Martello* led a comparatively uneventful life after entering service at New Cross in 1875. No. 32662, one of the last three Terriers' to be withdrawn, tended to accumulate more mileage than its sisters. It was used on the last day of services on the Hayling Island branch on November 2, 1963 but was still in occasional service in early 1964. It was sold to Butlins for static display at its holiday camp at Heads of Ayr in Scotland, leaving Eastleigh after restoration to LBSCR livery on September 2, and being put in position in October along with Stanier Pacific No. 6233 *Duchess of Sutherland*.

It was loaned to the museum at Bressingham Gardens in Norfolk in February 1971 along with the Duchess, and returned to steam in 1973, having been purchased by Bressingham. The locomotive remained there for several years in a shed before removal and full restoration, which commenced in the late 1990s. Still in Marsh umber livery numbered 662 with LBSC on the tanks, it has visited several heritage railways in the UK since being returned to traffic. In May 2011 it was repainted in BR black as 32662 with the late BR logo, at Loughborough on the Great Central Railway in readiness to join Nos. 32670 and 32678 on the K&ESR for the Last Train Commemoration that took place on June 11, 2011.

A1X 0-6-0T No. 32650

No. 50 *Whitechapel* was transferred by the Southern Railway to the Isle of Wight in 1930, becoming W9 *Fishbourne*. It quickly returned but became departmental No. 515S as Lancing carriage works pilot. In 1953 though, it became BR No. 32650 to work passenger services on the Hayling Island branch.

After withdrawal following closure of the branch in November 1963, it was purchased by London Borough of Sutton and Cheam; the originally intended purchase, No. 61 *Sutton,* having been cut up. The intention was to display the engine outside the new Civic Centre, but the engine was offered a home on the KESR until the work was completed and it arrived on April 19, 1964 after a two day journey under its own steam from Eastleigh. It was restored by 1966, carrying the KESR number 10 and named *Sutton* and used to haul the official opening train on the preserved KESR in 1974. It has seen regular service on the line, but after slipping down the overhaul queue at Rolvenden, the engine was moved to the Spa Valley Railway by the owners, Sutton Borough Council, and restoration work commenced.

A1X 0-6-0T W11 and E4 0-6-2T No. 473 near Smallbrook Junction on August 21, 1999.
HUGH BALLANTYNE

A1X 0-6-0T No. 11 *Newport*

No. 40 *Brighton* was exhibited in Paris in 1878 when new, running across France under its own steam. In January 1902, *Brighton* was sold to the Isle of Wight Central Railway for £600, becoming No. 11 in crimson lake livery, replaced by lined black in 1918. In SR days, W11 was named *Newport* in 1930. It returned to the mainland in 1947 but as No. 32640, was withdrawn from Brighton in September 1963 before the Hayling Island branch closed, having seen service there and on the KESR among other places.

Three members of the class were sold by BR to Butlins for display at holiday camps. Restored to yellow ochre livery at Eastleigh but with its BR front number plate, No. 32640 arrived at Pwllheli in July/August 1964, along with LMS Pacific No. 46203 *Princess Margaret Rose*.

Having been declared surplus by Butlins, it was initially loaned to the Isle of Wight Steam Railway, arriving in Ryde on January 27, 1973. It moved to Havenstreet on January 27, 1975 and was sold to the railway four years later for £35,000. A lengthy restoration was started in 1981 but not completed until the summer of 1989, and *Newport* continued to run until 2002 when it was again withdrawn for overhaul. The locomotive's boiler was found to be life-expired, and it was found cheaper to order a new boiler made (for £70,000) in 2007. In October 2010, the new boiler was delivered, and the locomotive will return to service in 2014.

A1X 0-6-0T No. 32640 in BR livery on April 27, 1996.
HUGH MADGIN

A1X 0-6-0T W8 *Freshwater*

No. 46 *Newington* has perhaps the most unusual history of any 'Terrier'; being sold to the LSWR where it became No. 734, intended for use on the Lyme Regis branch. It did not take to this duty, and after various other odd jobs, went on loan to the Freshwater Yarmouth & Newport Railway in 1913, being purchased in 1914 and given the number 2. The SR named it *Freshwater* in 1928 and renumbered it W8 in 1932. One of two 'Terriers' still on the island at Nationalisation, W8 returned to the mainland in 1949 and was soon put to work on the Hayling Island branch as No. 32646. It worked until 1963 but not right to the end and was stored at Eastleigh for 12 months after withdrawal.

It was sold to the Sadler Rail Coach Company based at Droxford, Hampshire on the disused Meon Valley Railway, where it arrived in late November 1964 under its own steam. It was used on occasions between the Droxford and Wickham stations on that line, but was sold to the Portsmouth-based Brickwoods brewery in the spring of 1966, moving on May 17 that year. The brewery had purchased it to act as an oversized pub sign outside a new public house to be opened on Hayling Island named The Hayling Billy. The engine was displayed there in Stroudley livery for a number of years, becoming locally famous, before being donated by Brickwoods' successor, Whitbread to the Isle of Wight

Steam Railway, moving on June 18, 1979.

On June 21, 1981, No. 8 *Freshwater,* in SR green livery, headed a train once again on the Isle of Wight, and has been in regular service, making occasional visits to railways on the mainland.

No. 8 *Freshwater* near Havenstreet on the IOWSR on November 26, 1983. JOHN WHITELEY

A1X 0-6-0T No. 32678

No. 78 *Knowle* entered service on July 23, 1880, one of the last eight of the class to be built.

For a short period in the early 1930s, it saw service on the lighter lines of the Isle of Wight, for which it was fitted with an extended bunker, becoming W4 (later W14) *Bembridge*.

On return to the mainland in 1936, it was reboilered and renumbered No. 2678 by the SR, joining the fleet of 'Terriers' used on the Hayling Island branch until 1940, when it was sent on what proved to be an extended loan to the KESR.

Apart from brief trips away, No. 32678 stayed at Rolvenden and, along with No. 32655, better known today as the Bluebell Railway's *Stepney,* shared in the working of the last passenger trains on January 2, 1954.

No. 32678 did not feature in the Hayling Island finale, being withdrawn a month earlier, and was sold to Butlin's for display at its holiday camp at Minehead alongside No. 6229 *Duchess of Hamilton*, arriving there in July 1964. When Butlins disposed of its engines, No. 78 was purchased by the West Somerset Railway in March 1975, but restoration proved impractical and it was resold to Rick Edmondson in 1983, moving to Resco's works at Woolwich where a lengthy restoration began.

It took many years to complete, moving to the KESR in July 1988 but No. 32678, now in BR lined black livery, was steamed in 1999 and so was in service in time to take part in the re-opening of the KESR extension from Northiam to Bodiam in April 2001.

Now wholly owned by The Terrier Trust, which purchased it

following an appeal in 2000 when the previous owner wished to sell, No. 32678 is a regular performer on the line.

In recent years, No. 32678 has paid visits to the Bluebell, Severn Valley, North Yorkshire Moors and Mid-Hants railways and most recently, the West Somerset Railway.

A1X 0-6-0T No. 32678 passes New Bridge signalbox on the approach to Pickering on the North Yorkshire Moors Railway in October 2004.

A1 0-6-0T No. 82 *Boxhill*

No. 82 *Boxhill* had remained as an A1, not having been rebuilt as an A1X and was among a number of engines transferred into departmental use, restored to original condition, painted in the Stroudley's yellow ochre livery and used as a Brighton works' shunter, numbered 380S and named after the works itself. It was replaced by 377S, formerly No. 35 *Morden*, in 1946.

But on withdrawal that year, *Boxhill* was restored by the Southern Railway to original condition at Lancing works for exhibitions, travelling round the system under its own steam. After Nationalisation, it continued to be displayed on various special occasions in the Southern Region, but after moving to Tweedmouth on April 27, 1958 for a period of storage, it was soon returned south for restoration at Eastleigh and display at the Museum of British Transport, Clapham from 1961. It moved to the National Railway Museum at York on April 9, 1975.

A1 0-6-0T No. 82 *Boxhill* in the British Transport Museum at Clapham in 1967. JOHN TITLOW

E1 0-6-0T No. 110 *Burgundy*

The LBSCR E class 0-6-0T was designed by William Stroudley in 1874 for short-distance goods and pilot duties. Numbering 78 in total and named after places from all across Europe, they were reclassified E1 by D E Marsh.

After 1894, they were replaced by R J Billinton's E3 and E4 radial 0-6-2Ts and withdrawals commenced as long ago as 1908. Under the SR, withdrawals continued during the 1920s, with some examples sold to industrial railways rather than scrapped.

Four E1s were also transferred to the Isle of Wight in 1932/3, renumbered W1-W4 and given names related to the island. Nevertheless, 30 were inherited by BR in 1948 but the last survivor, No. 32694, was withdrawn in July 1961.

No. 110 was built at Brighton in March 1877. Named *Burgundy,* it was allocated to Brighton depot. The locomotive was built with a copper-capped chimney, crosshead pump and wooden brake blocks. Around 1892, Westinghouse air brakes were fitted and by the mid-1890s, No. 110 was at Three Bridges.

An early withdrawal in February 1927, No. 110 was sold on April 5 of that year to the Cannock and Rugeley Colliery Company for £925. A new boiler to a different design was made and fitted by Bagnalls of Stafford, resulting in a change of appearance and an increase in power due to an increased boiler pressure from 140 to 175psi. At Cannock Wood Colliery, No.110 was renumbered as No. 9, using the inverted numberplate from No. 6, an 1876 engine which had been sold.

As CRC No. 9, the engine gave many years of good service and was used extensively on the trip workings to Hednesford Canal basin and the BR exchange sidings on the LNWR Cannock to Rugeley line.

Withdrawn for a second time in 1963, the engine was sold to the Railway Preservation Society and stored at Hednesford, Staffordshire, until June 29, 1970, when it was moved to the nearby Chasewater Railway. Never steamed and only cosmetically restored, it was eventually sold to three members of the East Somerset Railway led by Dick Bellchambers, arriving at Cranmore on September 11, 1978.

A general overhaul was commenced in 1986 and it was first steamed at Cranmore on July 19, 1992, before returning to service in 1993, in SR green livery and numbered 110. It pulled its first train in service on Sunday, October 24, of that year and in 1996 visited the Bristol Harbour Railway. Unfortunately, firebox problems resulted in No. 110 being prematurely withdrawn from traffic in 1997.

In 2012 a generous bequest to the Isle of Wight Steam Railway enabled the line to purchase No. 110 and commence the job of restoring it to steam. In return, LMS Ivatt 2-6-0 No. 46447 was to go to the ESR on loan. E1s were used on the island by the SR but this was not one of the engines involved, although it is expected to enter service as No. 2 *Yarmouth*.

In SR olive green livery, LBSCR E4 0-6-2T No. B473 passes Town Place Farm on the Bluebell Railway. NICK GILLIAM

E4 0-6-2T No. 473 *Birch Grove*

Although the first of Brighton's 0-6-2 'Radial' tanks was designed by William Stroudley, it was under his successor, Robert Billinton, that they became a series of designs for different types of traffic. The E4, with an intermediate driving wheel size, was the most flexible and most numerous class.

The 'Radial' tank refers the radial axle for the trailing wheel where, rather than the more conventional pivoted pony truck, the radial axle is set in curved hornguides in the main frames.

No. 473, in accordance with LBSCR practice, was named *Birch Grove*, after a town or village in the area, Birch Grove being a small hamlet just north of Horsted Keynes, and its residents, including one-time Prime Minister Harold Macmillan, would have used Horsted Keynes as their local station.

Initially painted in Stroudley's famous 'improved engine green', which was actually a golden ochre, it was reboiled by Marsh in 1912 with an I1-type boiler, and repainted in his dark umber livery, losing its name in the process.

Arriving on the Bluebell straight out of BR service on October 16, 1962, it was quickly repainted into the authentic Marsh umber livery, though with its name reinstated, and ran until 1971, by which time its boiler was in need of major repairs.

Its overhaul took many years, finally being completed in 1998 and in early 2005 it was repainted into BR black livery, in which guise it paid a visit to the Severn Valley Railway. Its next overhaul was started immediately on withdrawal in May 2008, and because of the good condition of its boiler, which had much work carried out a decade earlier, was completed in January 2010, the engine now carrying SR olive green livery.

The locomotive has also paid working visits to the Isle of Wight Steam Railway and the Mid-Hants Railway.

LEFT: E4 0-6-2T No. 32473 departs from Bewdley during a visit to the Severn Valley Railway on March 12, 2005.

BELOW: In Marsh umber livery, E4 0-6-2T No. 473 awaits departure from Horsted Keynes on October 26, 2003.

H2 4-4-2 No. 32424 *Beachy Head*

The LBSCR H2 class 4-4-2s were some of the best-known and most charismatic engines on the Brighton line, although few in number. They were designed when Marsh was officially locomotive superintendent, and were built in 1911-12.

The preservation of the Bluebell Railway dates back to the late 1950s and although the early revivalists would have liked to purchase as many engines of Brighton pedigree as possible, the priority was for small and affordable 0-6-0Ts, and the engine many would like to have seen saved, the last Atlantic, No. 32424 *Beachy Head,* had been scrapped at Eastleigh in 1958.

The chance discovery in 2000 of steam locomotive boilers at a joinery firm's premises in Maldon, Essex, raised the possibility of building engines around these boilers, and it was established that one was in fact from a Great Northern Railway large Atlantic, one of which, No. 251 is preserved in the National Collection.

The boilers on these engines are however so similar to the LBSCR ones, that plans were quickly formulated by the Bluebell Railway in 2000 for a reincarnation of no less than *Beachy Head* itself. The boiler was secured and fundraising commenced. The remains of a tender were located and acquired and the project was launched. In November 2004, the frames were ordered; the bogie frames arrived the following month and the main frames in 2005, at which point the locomotive became a reality.

In 2005, the tender frames were nearing completion and a start was made on constructing the shed which would house the locomotive while under construction, named Atlantic House.

The shed was completed in 2006, drilling of frames and hornguides continued and the driving wheel castings were delivered.

In 2007 the frames were erected and in the following year, components for the cylinders and valve chest were delivered, the frames riveted and forged billets for connecting and coupling rods were delivered. The bogie frames were assembled in 2009

The fabricated left hand cylinder, slide bars and part of the forward end of No. 32424, showing the state of build as at June 15, 2013. PHIL BARNES

A general view taken in Atlantic House on June 15, 2013. This shows the boiler which is ready for tubing and in front of it is one of the valve train assemblies, showing from the expansion link to the valves. The large brass item on the nearest table is the brake valve and the smaller items are mainly drain cocks. PHIL BARNES

and in 2010, the cylinders and valve chests were fabricated and the air brake cylinders completed, along with bogie and trailing wheelsets. In 2013, the cylinders were attached to the frames and the finished driving wheels delivered.

Progress has been dramatic and with all major parts now constructed, the day is not too far away when a Brighton Atlantic will steam along the much-extended Bluebell Railway after all.

MAP OF THE LONDON BRIGHTON & SOUTH COAST RAILWAY AND ISLE OF WIGHT RAILWAY SYSTEM

CHAPTER 7

London & South Western Railway

The largest of the SR constituent companies, the LSWR, was particularly progressive, being in direct competition with the mighty Great Western Railway over much of its main line mileage.

The London and South Western Railway's network extended from London to Plymouth via Salisbury and Exeter, with branches to Ilfracombe and Padstow, and via Southampton to Bournemouth and Weymouth. It also had many routes connecting towns in Hampshire and Berkshire, including Portsmouth and Reading. Its lines reached their most westerly point at Padstow 260 miles from Waterloo on completion of the North Cornwall Railway in March 1899, but the LSWR was in direct competition on the route to the south west with the broad gauge Great Western Railway.

The company's routes west of Exeter were known to railwaymen as The Withered Arm, allegedly because of the appearance of the route map of this part of the system. These lines were constructed to much lower engineering standards than the routes nearer London, with steeper gradients, fewer major bridges, tunnels or cuttings, a lower maximum axle loading and long stretches of single track.

Among significant achievements of the L&SWR were the electrification of suburban lines and the introduction of power signalling.

In 1913, the LSWR, under Sir Herbert Walker, formerly of the London and North Western Railway whose suburban lines he had electrified on a 630v DC fourth rail system, chose 630v DC third rail electrification for its suburban routes. Implementation was delayed by the First World War and the first LSWR electric service ran on October 20, 1915, between Waterloo and Wimbledon

Early LSWR passenger livery was yellow ochre/brown with the initials LSW on the tank or tender sides, but this was eventually superseded by the more familiar LSWR passenger sage green livery.

The LSWR's locomotive engineer Joseph Hamilton Beattie was born in Ireland on May 12, 1808, educated in Belfast and apprenticed to his father, a Derry architect. He moved to England in 1835 as assistant to Joseph Locke on the Grand Junction Railway and from 1837 on the London and Southampton Railway. He became carriage and wagon superintendent at Nine Elms and succeeded John Viret Gooch as locomotive engineer in 1850.

Initially he designed a series of singles, but the weight of the Southampton and Salisbury expresses led to the development of 2-4-0s. In addition he developed a series of 85 2-4-0 well tanks and 0-6-0s, and his locomotives were among the most efficient of the time. Three examples of his well-known design, the 0298 Class 2-4-0WTs, were in service for 88 years until 1962. He was succeeded by his son, William George Beattie, in 1871, but he was not a success in this post and was forced to resign in 1878.

William Adams, locomotive superintendent from 1878 to 1895, had held similar posts on the North London Railway and the Great Eastern Railway.

His father had been resident engineer of the East and West India Docks Company and he was apprenticed to his father's works. The railway surveyor Charles Vignoles had previously worked on the construction of the London dock basins and this association then secured a position for Adams as an assistant in his drawing office.

In 1848 Adams became assistant works manager for Philip Taylor, an ironfounder, millwright and former assistant to Marc Brunel. Fluent in French and Italian, Adams soon found himself effectively the superintendent engineer for the Royal Sardinian Navy.

On the LSWR, 524 locomotives were produced to his designs. He supervised the expansion of Nine Elms works and the transfer of the carriage and wagon works to Eastleigh. Among his best-known designs were the 'Radial' 4-4-2T and O2 0-4-4T.

Dugald Drummond, brother of the engineer Peter Drummond, previously worked for the North British Railway, LB&SCR and Caledonian Railway before joining the LSWR in 1895.

He had been foreman erector at the Lochgorm works, Inverness, of the Highland Railway under William Stroudley and followed Stroudley to the LBSCR in 1870. In 1875 he was appointed locomotive superintendent of the North British Railway.

In 1882 he moved to the Caledonian Railway, but in April 1890 he tendered his resignation to enter business, establishing the Australasian Locomotive Engine Works at Sydney, New South Wales, Australia. Drummond accepted the post as locomotive engineer of the London and South Western Railway in 1895, working as chief mechanical engineer until his death in 1912. He will be particularly remembered for his T9 4-4-0 and M7 0-4-4T.

The LSWR's last chief mechanical engineer was Robert Wallace Urie. After working for various private locomotive manufacturers, Urie joined the Caledonian Railway in 1890 and became chief draughtsman and later works manager at St Rollox works in Glasgow under Dugald Drummond. In 1897 he moved with Drummond to join the LSWR as works manager at Nine Elms, transferring to the new works at Eastleigh in 1909.

Following Drummond's death in 1912, Urie became chief mechanical engineer until his own retirement at the Grouping of 1923.

Robert Urie was a respected locomotive engineer and made a significant contribution to the development of more powerful express passenger and goods locomotives for the LSWR; in particular his H15, N15 and S15 4-6-0s continued to be built by the Southern Railway under Richard Maunsell''s direction after the Grouping.

An LSWR doubleheader on the LSWR as the Drummond combination of M7 0-4-4T No. 30053 and T9 4-4-0 No. 120 depart from Herston on the Swanage Railway on October 17, 1992.

T3 4-4-0 No. 563

Twenty T3 4-4-0s, designed by Adams, were constructed in 1892-93.

All passed to the Southern Railway at the Grouping in 1923, but withdrawals started in 1930, and by the end of 1933 only three remained. The last, No. 563, was retired in August 1945 and set aside for preservation. It moved around the country during the late 1940s and 1950s, even as far north as Tweedmouth, and occasionally appearing at exhibitions. In January 1961 it was put on display in the Museum of British Transport at Clapham but was moved by rail to York in 1974 to take its place in the National Railway Museum. Its permanent home is now at Locomotion; the National Railway Museum at Shildon. It has never steamed in preservation.

ABOVE: T3 class 4-4-0 No. 563 in the Museum of British Transport at Clapham in 1967. JOHN TITLOW

RIGHT: T3 4-4-0 No. 563 in the National Railway Museum at York.

0298 class 2-4-0WT

The LSWR 0298 class or Beattie well tanks were built between 1863 and 1875 for London suburban branch lines, a total of 85 being built, designed by Joseph Beattie and built by Beyer Peacock in Manchester. They handled heavy loads and were fast runners, but from 1890, they were sent to depots outside the London area, and most were withdrawn between 1888 and 1890.

Six were modernised for use on branch lines in the south-west but three of these were withdrawn by 1898. Their appearance changed beyond all recognition. Joseph Beattie's design had an open footplate and a most unusual design of firebox with two fireholes, but the 1890s rebuild by William Adams featured a new boiler and an enclosed cab. A Drummond boiler was introduced during a later rebuild and the mechanical water pumps were removed, giving the appearance we are familiar with today.

The three survivors, Nos. 298, 314 and 329 were transferred to the Bodmin and Wadebridge branch in 1895, which was one of the earliest railways in Cornwall and had been isolated from the rest of the LSWR network until that year. Well suited to the sharp curves of the china clay branch to Wenford Bridge, despite numerous attempts to find suitable replacements, these three remained in service until they were finally withdrawn in 1962 after transfer to the Western Region of BR. They represented the oldest design still in use on BR by 1958, although of course substantially rebuilt.

0298 class 2-4-0WT No. 30585

Having covered 1,314,838 miles in its 89-year career, No. 30585 was purchased from BR in 1963 through the efforts of a handful of members of the London Railway Preservation Society. The Bluebell Railway had failed to secure the locomotive, but LRPS secretary Richard Castle approached BR for a quote for the purchase and was given a figure of £750. By October 14, 1963, the fund stood at £47-4s-7d, but BR demanded the £750 within one month. An extension was negotiated to the end of December and a cheque posted on deadline day.

In March 1964, No. 30585 was towed as freight to the Hockerill Cold Store, Bishops Stortford, before being transferred to Quainton Road on May 9, 1969, where a steam centre was being established which would eventually become the Buckinghamshire Railway Centre. The engine was returned to steam on March 22, 1970, and then worked passenger trains in the down yard for a number of years. In the 1980s major repairs became necessary and the engine was withdrawn from service.

Work began on giving the locomotive a major overhaul in 1999.

No. 30585's sister engine No. 30587, which was part of the National Railway Museum's collection, was restored to operation at the Flour Mill in the Forest of Dean. It was then based at the Bodmin & Wenford Railway. During 2005, No. 30585 followed it through the overhaul process, also at the Flour Mill.

Its first steaming after restoration took place on Saturday, October 7, 2006 at Quainton Road, with an official relaunch by Sir William McAlpine. A week later it left for Bodmin, as part of the restoration agreement, being reunited with its sister. The two locomotives operated together for the first time since hauling an enthusiast's special in the London area in 1962.

In January 2007 No. 30585 returned from Bodmin to Quainton, although further return trips to Cornwall will occur over the next few years. It has visited other railways, including the Mid-Hants, Swanage and Great Central railways, and even appeared at the Isle of Wight Steam Railway's gala in 2011.

0298 class 2-4-0WT No. 30587

No. 30587 was understandably chosen to be part of the National Collection and after storage at Fratton, moved to Stratford on September 12, 1964, then Preston Park in March 1968.

It was not put on display until loaned to the Dart Valley Railway (later the South Devon Railway), where it was on show in the museum at Buckfastleigh in LSWR green livery.

Its real salvation though, came with its overhaul in 2001-02 by Bill Parker at his Flour Mill workshop in the Forest of Dean, sponsored by Bodmin's Alan Moore. The engine was moved from Buckfastleigh in December 2001 and worked its first trains on the Bodmin & Wenford Railway in November 2002.

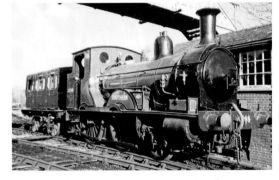

ABOVE: Returning to service after 40 years, 0298 class 2-4-0WT No. 30587 heads a Sentimental Journeys china clay photo charter at Charlie's Gate on the Bodmin & Wenford Railway on November 29, 2002.

LEFT: No. 3298 sees the light of day at Buckfastleigh on December 1, 2002, prior to movement to the Flour Mill for overhaul. BILL PARKER

Closer to its London suburban roots, No. 30587 stands at Baker Street on the Circle Line at 3am on Sunday, February 26, 2012 during test running in connection with the Metropolitan Railway 150th anniversary event.
ROBIN JONES

In BR black, Adams 'Radial' 4-4-2T No. 30583 departs from Sheffield Park on the Bluebell Railway on May 11, 1983.

Adams Radial 415 class 4-4-2T No. 488

No. 488 probably has the most interesting history of all the preserved Southern steam engines.

The class was designed in 1882 by William Adams to accelerate LSWR suburban services. Adams preferred a large-wheeled engine with a front bogie to the 0-4-4Ts which dominated suburban trains on many railways. It used the 'radial' design of rear axle and 71 were built in total, all by four outside contractors.

However Drummond's M7 0-4-4Ts soon displaced the 0415s and after service on country branch lines, class members saw a variety of unusual duties during the First World War, some were even used in Scotland on the Highland Railway, but most were scrapped around the end of the war.

In September 1917, No. 0488 was sold to the Ministry of Munitions, for use at Ridham dock near Sittingbourne, but was sold in March 1923 for £375 to Colonel Stephens, to run on the East Kent Railway. As a passenger engine, it was not suited to hauling coal trains and was little used, but still lasted 20 years on the EKR.

Having a short wheelbase and guiding bogies, the 4-4-2Ts were well suited to tight curves, resulting in the class being noted for its long service on the Lyme Regis branch, where it had been introduced in 1903 after beating an O2 0-4-4T and a Stroudley 'Terrier' 0-6-0T in trials.

The last two members of the class in SR stock, Nos. 0125 and 0520, were retired in 1929, but their LBSCR replacements proved unsatisfactory and the last two 0415s were overhauled to carry on at Lyme Regis after all. Amazingly the SR decided in 1946 that a third would be useful and found No. 488 out of use on the EKR. Purchased for £120, the engine was overhauled and returned to traffic.

It was only track modifications on the branch which enabled BR to finally replace the three 0415s at Lyme Regis in 1961, although DMUs soon took over and the line closed in 1964.

No. 30583, the one-time No. 488, once on the EKR, was purchased by the Bluebell Railway, being selected as it retained the original design of boiler.

Arriving on the line under its own steam on July 12, 1961, and entering traffic immediately, it was a very regular performer until 1990, and has carried both LSWR green and BR black liveries. Withdrawn in 1990, it requires extensive overhaul, almost certainly involving replacement of the boiler barrel.

In LSWR green livery, 4-4-2T No. 488 is seen near Holywell on the Bluebell Railway on February 26, 1989.

O2 0-4-4T No. 24 *Calbourne*

No. 209 was one of 60 O2 0-4-4Ts built by the LSWR in 1891 at Nine Elms, and was originally based at Fratton before moving on to Exeter.

The class was designed for London suburban services, replacing the Beattie well tanks, but began to be replaced as early as 1897 by the introduction of the more powerful Drummond M7s and T1s. The O2s were cascaded to lighter services, and became distributed throughout the LSWR system, being of particular use on restricted branch lines.

The class is usually associated with the Isle of Wight railway system, where the final two O2s were sent over in 1949, after Nationalisation, resulting in a total of 23 locomotives on the island being fitted with Westinghouse air brake equipment and an extended coal bunker. The class proved to be ideal for the island's railways.

Locomotives on the island were renumbered in a separate sequence with the prefix 'W' and taking the next available number, or the number of the withdrawn locomotive they were sent over to replace. Eventually those on the island occupied the entire sequence between W14 and W36. They were all named after places on the island.

No. 209 was transferred to the Isle of Wight on April 26, 1925, renumbered W24 and given the name *Calbourne*. The last of the mainland O2s was No. 30225, withdrawn in 1962.

The O2s were synonymous with the Isle of Wight throughout BR steam days and No. 24 was retained after steam services ended, with No. 31 *Chale,* as a works engine for the Ryde to Shanklin line electrification, until withdrawal in March 1967 when electrification of the line was complete.

Calbourne was acquired along with two SECR carriages and three ex-LBSCR vehicles. by the Wight Locomotive Society in 1967, to become the flagship locomotive of the Isle of Wight Steam Railway. The wildlife artist David Shepherd put £500 into the funds to bring the total much nearer the £900 required for the locomotive.

On purchase, the locomotive was stranded at Ryde with the Cowes line being severed, but on August 15, 1969, it was moved by road to join its train at Newport and work started in earnest to make it operational.

Returned to steam in November 1970, *Calbourne* steamed with its train from Newport to its new home at Havenstreet where the embryonic Isle of Wight Steam Railway was being established, on October 24, 1971, during the BR steam ban which

was not lifted until 12 months later. Initially running in SR green livery, it was withdrawn in 2002 for overhaul, emerging in 2010 in BR black livery with the larger bunker refitted.

The extensive repairs were supported by a Heritage Lottery Fund grant and included a major boiler and firebox overhaul, and a new smokebox.

The locomotive resumed its place as flagship of the IOWSR fleet, and made visits to railways on the mainland in 2012.

In SR green livery, LSWR O2 0-4-4T W24 *Calbourne* departs from Havenstreet on September 3, 1991. HUGH MADGIN

LSWR O2 0-4-4T No. 24 *Calbourne* and resident Beattie 2-4-0WT No. 30587 climb past Pendewey Farm with the 3.34pm Boscarne Junction to Bodmin General during *Calbourne's* visit to the Bodmin & Wenford Railway for its Spring Steam Spectacular gala of April 20-22, 2012. CLASSIC TRACTION

LSWR O2 0-4-4T No. 24 *Calbourne* is seen in BR black livery near Woodhouse Farm crossing on the Isle of Wight Steam Railway with a private charter of 1950s red-liveried stock on November 5, 2012. JOHN WHITELEY

B4 0-4-0T

The B4 was Adams' design of standard dock shunting engine. In 1891 the LSWR obtained control of most of the port of Southampton, its major source of goods traffic. To replace the collection of ancient tank engines, a further 10 B4s were constructed at Nine Elms.

The B4s were eventually replaced by the war surplus USA 0-6-0Ts in 1947. They still had stovepipe chimneys at this time but the cabs had been enclosed as air raid precautions. Many of the class were withdrawn but a couple were retained and their last duty was shunting in Winchester goods yard where Nos. 30096 and 30102 worked until withdrawn in 1963.

B4 0-4-0T No. 96 *Normandy*

On withdrawal, No. 30096 was sold for industrial service at fuel merchants Corralls, at Dibles wharf, Northam, Southampton.

As *Corrall Queen* No. 30096 put in nine years more hard work before being sold in 1972 to a group of enthusiasts, many of whom were members of the Bulleid Society. The engine was delivered to Sheffield Park on December 18. An overhaul was started in the late 1970s, but progressed slowly and the engine

RIGHT: No. 96 is unusually seen in passenger service on the Bluebell Railway, hauling the Metropolitan Chesham set past the waterworks on February 22, 2003. DAVID FRANKLIN

B4 0-4-0T No. 102 *Granville* on display at Bressingham.

was not steamed until May 1986, fully restored to Adams goods green, a much darker shade than used on passenger engines. Fitted with a vacuum ejector it quickly found plenty of employment on pilot use, works and goods trains, and especially the regular Monday carriage works shunt at Horsted Keynes, thought to be Europe's last regular non-passenger steam operation.

The boiler certificate expired in 2006 and *Normandy* is now stored awaiting overhaul.

B4 0-4-0T No. 102 *Granville*

The other B4 to survive at Winchester, No. 30102, was purchased by Butlins and put on display in September 1963 at its holiday camp at Skegness, in the company of LMS 4-6-0 No. 6100 *Royal Scot* no less.

An eventual change of policy, particularly in view of the deteriorating external condition of the locomotives, saw all of Butlins' steam engines dispersed to various preservation sites, Bressingham Gardens in Norfolk being particularly favoured. No. 102 arrived there on March 16, 1971. It was restored to dark green livery and given its name *Granville*.

Working on the LSWR, B4 0-4-0T No. 96 *Normandy* departs from Herston in the early days of operations on the Swanage Railway on July 12, 1987.

M7 0-4-4T

The M7 0-4-4Ts were built between 1897 and 1911, the first type to be designed by Dugald Drummond and largely intended to replace smaller Adams-designed 0-4-4Ts on LSWR London suburban services.

The first 25 were constructed at Nine Elms between March and November 1897, and were built in five batches, each with major variations in design; 105 were built and many were fitted for push-pull operation.

It was the heaviest 0-4-4T ever to run in Britain, and was a development of Drummond's earlier designs for the NBR and LBSCR. The boiler, cylinders and motion were identical and interchangeable with Drummond's 700 class 0-6-0 and the boiler was used on his C8 4-4-0.

Somewhat ambitiously, the LSWR initially allocated M7s to work semi-fast passenger services between London and Portsmouth,

Exeter and Plymouth and Bournemouth and Weymouth, but they were quickly withdrawn from these duties after a high speed derailment near Tavistock in 1898.

As newer engines came into service and more suburban lines were electrified, the class became more confined to branch line operation across the SR system, including former SECR routes, and in BR days, LBSCR routes.

Apart from one experimental engine, all the M7s passed into BR service, but No. 672 quickly fell down the lift shaft which provided rolling stock access to the Waterloo and City Line, and was cut up.

They maintained their association with the capital, working empty trains between Clapham Junction and Waterloo, but withdrawals started in 1957 and by the end of 1963, the majority of survivors were based at Bournemouth to work the Swanage branch.

M7 0-4-4T No. 245 in the National Railway Museum at York.

No. 245 with No. 30850 *Lord Nelson* at Stewarts Lane in the course of transfer from Preston Park to York in 1977.
JOHN TITLOW

M7 0-4-4T No. 245

No. 245 was constructed in 1897 at the cost of £1846.

Then the oldest surviving M7, No. 30245, was selected for preservation as part of the National Collection in November 1962.

Like most SR National Collection engines, it spent a period in store at Fratton until moved to Stratford works on September 12, 1964. However, it was painted LSWR green on one side for a filming assignment but still not put on display and moved with most of the other Stratford engines, to Preston Park on February 12, 1968. It was not moved to York until 1977, and was repainted at Derby in 1981 since when it has been on display in the National Railway Museum apart from a period at the Mid-Hants Railway in 1988-90. It has never been steamed in preservation.

In LSWR days the M7s carried various liveries but the one associated with the class was passenger light sage green livery with purple-brown edging, creating panels of green. This was further lined in white and black with 'LSWR' in gilt on the tank sides, and the number on the bunker sides. Interestingly, the National Railway Museum has chosen a less typical green for the livery on No. 245.

ABOVE: Running on the main line as No. 30673, LSWR M7 0-4-4T No. 30053 arrives at Salisbury from Eastleigh on June 28, 1992.

OPPOSITE RIGHT: No. 30053 and T9 4-4-0 No. 30120 cross Corfe Common on the Swanage Railway on March 16 2014.

M7 0-4-4T No. 30053

No. 53, built in 1905, was based at Bournemouth for a few months in early 1964 and worked the Swanage branch along with the 'Old Road' from Poole to Brockenhurst via Wimborne and Ringwood. It was withdrawn along with the last few remaining M7s at Bournemouth in mid-May 1964.

The locomotive was then cosmetically restored at Eastleigh before being sold to a major steam museum in the United States, known as Steamtown at Bellows Falls, Vermont, being shipped out in company with SR Schools class 4-4-0 No. 926 *Repton* in 1967.

M7 0-4-4T No. 30053 pilots Bulleid Pacific No. 34105 *Swanage* on the Swanage Railway on March 19, 1993.

The museum's owner, F Nelson Blount died and Steamtown relocated to Scranton, Pennsylvania, in 1986. However, the two British engines were not required by the museum and the M7 was successfully repatriated by the Drummond Locomotive Society in 1987, initially on the Swanage Railway, arriving from Felixstowe docks on April 9.

No. 30053 is now in the ownership of Drummond Locomotives Ltd, which acquired the assets of The Drummond Locomotive Society in 1988.

It moved to Swindon works in 1988 where its overhaul commenced, but then to the East Anglian Railway Museum at Chappell & Wakes Colne in Essex in December 1990, where work continued until it was steamed in December 1991, making its first runs on May 19, 1992.

Its use was limited at Chappell though and it returned to Swanage on June 4, 1992, where it has since operated regularly.

It has frequently visited other lines and even briefly held a main line certificate, hauling a coach and brakevan from Eastleigh to Salisbury in June 1992.

No. 30053 underwent another heavy overhaul in 2007, including a set of new tyres, and ran for some years in SR black livery as No. 53, visiting railways such as the Bodmin & Wenford.

A rare sight as No. 30053 pilots LMS Princess Coronation Pacific No. 46233 *Duchess of Sutherland* away from Dereham on the Mid-Norfolk Railway in July 2013.

M7 0-4-4T No. 30053 shunts stock at Swanage on March 19, 1993.

T9 4-4-0 No. 30120

Drummond introduced the T9 4-4-0 in 1899 for express passenger work in south-west England and 66 were eventually built, in fact an order of 50 was placed straight off the drawing board. Large fireboxes and Stephenson link valve gear ensured a free-steaming locomotive.

Construction was shared between Nine Elms works and Dübs and Co of Glasgow; 20 at Nine Elms and 30 by Dübs. The last batch was given the Drummond 'watercart' eight-wheel tender for longer running between water stops, later provided for all class members.

Robert Urie supplied the class with superheaters and from 1922 the entire class was equipped, together with further minor modifications.

The T9s were popular with their crews, and were quickly given the nickname 'Greyhounds' in view of their liking for fast running. Livery was Drummond's LSWR passenger sage green, with purple-brown edging and black and white lining.

The class was haphazardly numbered by the LSWR. The Nine Elms batch was numbered 113 to 122 and 280 to 289, while the Glasgow batch was allocated 702 to 719 and 721 to 732, and the final Glasgow locomotive, No. 773. The haphazard numbering was perpetuated by the SR and BR.

The class remained intact throughout SR days and 20 still remained on BR's books in 1959, by then being used on lighter duties in the west country.

The last survivor, No. 30120, was withdrawn from Exmouth Junction in October 1961 but remained in capital stock. In March 1962 it was outshopped from Eastleigh works following a heavy casual repair and returned to service in LSWR green working ordinary services as well as railtours. It was withdrawn from capital stock in July 1963 but continued to work special trains until October of that year.

Following lengthy periods in store at Fratton and Stratford, it

In SR green livery, T9 4-4-0 No. 120 and S15 4-6-0 No. 506 depart from Alton on the Mid-Hants Railway on June 19, 1988.

joined most of the unrestored National Collection locomotives at Preston Park on February 19, 1968, but was placed on loan to the Birmingham Railway Museum at Tyseley, arriving on September 7, 1970, where it remained as a static exhibit until moved to the National Railway Museum at York in November 1977.

It was never put on display at York but was loaned to the Mid-Hants Railway, arriving on September 18, 1981, where it was overhauled and returned to steam in May 1983 in BR black livery. It was repainted into SR green livery but it was not suited to the line's steep gradients and moved to the Swanage Railway on December 14, 1990, where it remained until its boiler certificate expired in 1993.

It then moved to the Bluebell Railway on March 25, 1994, but it was never felt practicable to return it to steam and it remained as a static exhibit until February 1, 2008.

It moved yet again, to the Bodmin and Wenford Railway, and was returned to steam in August 2010 back in BR black livery following a heavy overhaul including repairs to the cylinder block at Bill Parker's Flour Mill Workshop in the Forest of Dean, sponsored by Bodmin benefactor Alan Moore.

No. 30120 remains a part of the National Collection but on long term loan to the Bodmin and Wenford Railway, from where it has paid short visits to other preserved railways including the Mid-Hants.

Back in service after overhaul by Bill Parker at the Flour Mill workshops, T9 4-4-0 No. 30120 is seen near Boscarne Junction on the Bodmin & Wenford Railway on September 2, 2010.

L&B 2-6-2T No. 190 *Lyd* departs from Porthmadog with a train for Blaenau Ffestiniog.

Lynton & Barnstaple 2-6-2T No. 190 *Lyd*

By a happy coincidence, the Lynton & Barnstaple Railway ran to the same 1ft 11½in gauge as the preserved Ffestiniog Railway, and at around the same time as the revival of the L&B started to bear fruit with the restoration of Woody Bay station and the commencement of tracklaying, FR general manager Paul Lewin commenced an ambitious project to build a new 2-6-2T to the L&B Manning-Wardle design for eventual use on the Ffestiniog.

The new locomotive was completed in 2010/11 and commenced running-in on the FR, but it was quickly hired to the L&B for a weekend in May 2011, bringing back the sight of an L&B 2-6-2T to Exmoor, though still in plain black livery in accordance with the FR's tradition for new engines being run-in.

It entered regular service on the FR numbered 30190 in BR lined black livery, as L&B engines may have appeared had it not been closed by the SR in 1935, and ran on the newly-completed Welsh Highland Railway in this guise. Having been repainted into SR green livery numbered 190 and named *Lyd,* it made a further appearance on the L&B in May 2013, where it was able to haul two newly-restored L&B coaches, which had been rebuilt after many years' use as chicken sheds.

This resulted in an authentic L&B train on L&B metals, a sight no-one could have predicted as the Southern steam revival was in full swing in the 1980s and 1990s.

In fictitious BR black livery, L&B 2-6-2T No. 30190 *Lyd* acting as station pilot for Welsh Highland Railway services at Porthmadog on the Ffestiniog Railway.

L&B 2-6-2T No. 190 *Lyd* heads a train of two L&B coaches towards Woody Bay on the Lynton & Barnstaple Railway in May 2013.

MAP OF THE LONDON & SOUTH WESTERN RAILWAY AND SOMERSET & DORSET JOINT RAILWAY

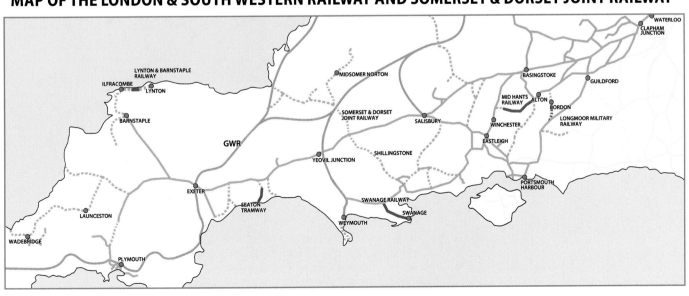

S15 4-6-0

The LSWR S15 4-6-0 was designed by Robert Urie, based on his H15 and N15 4-6-0s. There were interchangeable parts, although a taper boiler was used on the S15 and N15s, as opposed to the parallel boiler of the H15s. Construction ran from 1920 to 1936, the first in LSWR days, which used them on freight trains to the south coast ports and to Exeter, as well as occasional passenger work.

The first chief mechanical engineer of the Southern Railway, Richard Maunsell, later increased the strength to 45 locomotives, with modifications to the loading gauge, allowing a wider route availability.

The benefits gained by Maunsell's modifications showed in the improved performance of the first batch of Maunsell S15s over their Urie-built predecessors. Maunsell had taken a sound design and made it better, achieving a consistent locomotive capable of undertaking all the tasks for which it was intended. A final modification was when all locomotives were equipped with smoke deflectors, a feature that was eventually to apply to most larger Maunsell-influenced designs.

Both Urie and Maunsell S15s spent most of their working lives on the Southern Railway's Western section, No. 30837 being the final member of the class in operation, returning to Feltham in January 1966 to work a farewell railtour.

S15 4-6-0 No. 30499 undergoing heavy overhaul at Ropley on the Mid-Hants Railway in July 2013 alongside SR-built No. 828.

S15 4-6-0 No. 30499

No. 499 is the oldest surviving S15, having been one of the first batch of five ordered in January 1916. It was not completed at Eastleigh until May 1920, when it was allocated to Nine Elms for heavy goods work. It was reallocated to Feltham in 1940 where it joined the rest of the class. In 1931, E499 had received Maunsell lined green livery and smoke deflectors, reverting back to No. 499 in 1934.

However, it spent the early war years working for the GWR out of Old Oak Common. At the end of 1963, No. 30499 lost its original Urie double bogie 5000 gallon tender for an Ashford six-wheel 4000 gallon one, but a few days later it was condemned, with 1.24 million miles on the clock. From storage at Feltham, No. 30499 started its last journey to Woodham's scrapyard at Barry in June 1964.

The engine languished at Barry for 16 years before losing its tender again, when it was purchased to go with class U class 2-6-0 No. 31625, which left for the Mid-Hants Railway in 1980. The aim of the Urie Locomotive Society was to preserve an S15 4-6-0 for operation, and the society now owns the only two surviving Urie S15s, Nos. 30499 and 30506, built for the LSWR in 1920 at Eastleigh.

The society had already purchased sister engine No. 30506 in 1973 and moved it to the MHR, and the idea was to purchase No. 30499 as a full set of spare parts, but after arriving at Ropley on November 10, 1983, the intention was to eventually return it to steam. A Maunsell double bogie 5000 gallon tender was also purchased from Barry, and in 1996, No. 30499 was taken to Riley & Son Engineering's workshops at Bury, where its boiler was donated to No. 30506. No. 30499's frames were overhauled and painted, and it moved back to the MHR where after a period of storage., restoration has now recommenced.

S15 4-6-0 No. 506

No. 506 was ordered in March 1917, but not completed at Eastleigh until October 1920 and went to Nine Elms then on to Feltham in 1923, when the new marshalling yard was opened.

The Urie Locomotive Society was formed in April 1972 and No. 30506 was purchased from Barry scrapyard in March 1973 for £4000. It arrived on the Mid-Hants Railway on April 30, 1976, but it was discovered that its boiler was beyond repair and the society purchased the boiler from No. 30825 at Barry, which was fitted in

No. 30506 undergoing restoration in the open air at Ropley on the Mid-Hants Railway on July 3, 1977 soon after the line had been reopened.

S15 4-6-0 No. 506 heads towards Medstead & Four Marks on the Mid-Hants Railway on January 22, 1989.

February 1981. This resulted in No. 506 eventually returning to steam in the summer of 1987, being launched into traffic in Southern green in October and running on the MHR for 14 years before withdrawal in 2001. Its period of operation had been extended when it received the boiler from sister engine No. 499.

During its period of operation, the locomotive has seen a repaint into BR black livery and has visited other railways including the East Lancashire Railway.

A further overhaul is under way with extensive repairs having been completed in the new boiler workshop at Ropley.

Meanwhile the chassis has been moved into the workshops where considerable attention is focusing on the front end where the bufferbeam has been removed for replacement and the cylinders are now under investigation for removal to attend to corrosion in the areas between the frames and the cylinder blocks. A return to steam is expected in the near future.

In BR black, S15 4-6-0 No. 30506 passes Burrs on the East Lancashire Railway on August 30, 1993.

CHAPTER 8

The Southern Railway

In mileage terms the smallest of the 'Big Four', the Southern developed a unique style of its own which was to last right to the end of steam 20 years after Nationalisation.

The Grouping of the numerous independent railway companies into the 'Big Four' took effect from January 1, 1923, and one of the new companies was the Southern Railway.

The three major constituents of the SR were of course the South Eastern & Chatham Railway, the London Brighton & South Coast Railway and the London & South Western Railway. Many smaller independent companies were absorbed such as the Plymouth Devonport & South Western Junction Railway and of course the Isle of Wight lines, but not Colonel Stephens' East Kent or Kent & East Sussex railways.

From a locomotive point of view it was the appointment of Richard Maunsell, formerly of the SECR which was to shape the future development of SR motive power.

The SR was subdivided into three sections, Eastern, Central and Western, following the boundaries of the three major constituent companies which had surprisingly little overlap of territory. The SR bordered the Great Western Railway on its northern side but was physically almost totally separate from the LMS and LNER, although the Somerset & Dorset line, formerly jointly owned by the LSWR and Midland Railway continued to be

jointly owned by the SR and LMS, running right through GWR territory. Motive power was predominantly LMS though.

West of Exeter, the SR and GWR were in even more direct competition, the SR serving north Devon and Cornwall, with its ex-LSWR routes, while the GWR served the south of the two counties.

On January 1, 1948, the Southern Railway became the Southern Region of British Railways, with no change to its routes or boundaries, except that some minor lines were absorbed at this stage, including the Kent & East Sussex Railway.

The major change to the Southern Region came about in 1962/3 when all SR routes west of Exeter were transferred to the Western Region, finally ending the overlapping of routes in Devon and Cornwall. The WR was far more advanced with dieselisation in the area than the SR and SR steam power west of Exeter was quickly replaced by WR diesel-hydraulic traction

SR steam was now in retreat but famously the Bulleid Pacifics especially, remained in top-link express service right up to July 1967, working the Waterloo-Weymouth and Salisbury routes, Britain's last steam main line.

Face to face at Eastleigh works are Southern malachite green-liveried 4-6-0 No. 850 *Lord Nelson* and the ultimate in Southern steam, rebuilt Merchant Navy Pacific No. 35005 *Canadian Pacific*.

Richard Maunsell

On Grouping in 1923, Maunsell became the Southern Railway's first chief mechanical engineer. He had initially built few significant designs for the South Eastern & Chatham Railway, but rebuilt some Wainwright Es as E1s and Ds as D1s, making them more powerful but considerably less stylish in the process.

However, the SECR's light axle load limit precluded the use of big engines, but Maunsell's new designs were the 5ft 7in driving wheel N class 2-6-0s and the 6ft driving wheel R (River) class 2-6-4Ts. The tanks proved to be unstable at speed and were rebuilt in SR days as 2-6-0 tender engines and classified as U, effectively an N but with 6ft driving wheels.

When Maunsell became the CME of the SR, his priority was to design a standardised range of locomotives that were suitable to operate on all three of the SR's sections, which varied greatly in terms of loading gauge and quality of permanent way. He also attempted to design as few types as possible.

While engineer Robert Urie on the LSWR had built a series of 4-6-0s, the S15, H15 and the N15 (King Arthurs), Maunsell continued building his SECR 2-6-0s for mixed traffic use and Urie's LSWR 4-6-0s for freight, but quickly made a name for himself with a huge four-cylinder express 4-6-0, the Lord Nelson.

In one way it followed contemporary Swindon practice in that it had four cylinders but there the similarity ended. This was brute force as against Swindon sophistication and elegance. Sir Henry Fowler on the LMS, desperate for a big express engine, virtually copied the design for his Royal Scot 4-6-0, but with three cylinders. The Scots were rebuilt into more of the GW-influenced design criteria later adopted by Stanier on the LMS, with a taper boiler, but the Nelsons stayed in their original form and made an interesting comparison with the rebuilt Scots in BR days.

Perhaps Maunsell's greatest success was the Schools class 4-4-0, a scaled-down Lord Nelson, but the most powerful 4-4-0 to run in Europe.

Maunsell retired in November 1937, to be succeeded by Bulleid, following which, major changes ensued in the direction of the SR's motive power policy, and locomotive livery.

Two Maunsell locomotives at Horsted Keynes on the Bluebell Railway in June 1981; U class 2-6-0 No. 1618 and Schools class 4-4-0 No. 928 *Stowe*.

LOCOMOTIVE NUMBERING

Until 1931, the Southern Railway initially maintained the locomotive numbers from its constituents, and solved the problem of more than one locomotive having the same number by prefixing SECR locomotives with 'A' for Ashford, LBSCR by 'B' for Brighton and LSWR engines by 'E' for Eastleigh). New locomotives were prefixed by the letter of the works where they were built. All three major companies had rather haphazard numbering systems in any case. In 1931 the fleet was renumbered by dropping the prefixes and adding 1000 to all SECR engines and 2000 to all LBSCR engines, while leaving LSWR engines with their original numbers.

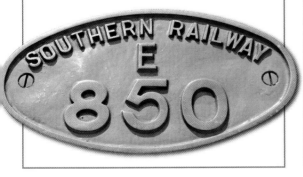

LIVERY

After Grouping in 1923, locomotives were outshopped in Richard Maunsell's darker version of the LSWR sage green livery, generally referred to as olive green, with black and white lining and yellow lettering.

With the appointment of Bulleid as chief mechanical engineer in 1937, livery policy was changed to malachite green for passenger locomotives, lined with yellow and black with solid black edging and with sunshine yellow lettering .

Goods engines were painted black and some classes remained in olive green but with the 'Southern' lettering changed to the sunshine yellow style. The LSWR painted locomotives in sage green as adopted by Urie during the First World War but the exact shade varied and this was continued by Maunsell after Grouping, but coaches were a darker 'Parson's green' and Maunsell adopted this for locomotives in 1925/26, becoming known as Maunsell green. In 1936, in response to changes in public taste, Maunsell painted engines a brighter shade of green, mid/light olive, but it was found not to wear well.

Although there is a story that Sir Herbert Walker before he retired chose malachite green and therefore Bulleid was committed to it, it is generally accepted that Bulleid chose malachite. The board thought it too bright and although Bulleid agreed to tone it down a bit, in reality he did not.

S15 4-6-0 No. 825 departs from Goathland on the North Yorkshire Moors Railway on December 29, 2005.

S15 4-6-0 No. 825

The oldest surviving SR-built S15 had lost its boiler to No. 30506 but its frames were moved from Barry to the premises of Steam & Sail Ltd at Brightlingsea, Essex in November 1986. Following the failure of this venture, the remains of the engine were moved to the North Yorkshire Moors Railway in 1990. The frames were used to replace the twisted and cracked ones of sister engine No. 841 and in accordance with SR practice, when the locomotive returned to steam, it carried the number of the frames, 825.

In more familiar guise, complete with smoke deflectors, No. 825 heads past Water Ark with LNER teak coaching stock.

S15 4-6-0 No. 828 'Harry H Frith'

S15 No. 828 was built at Eastleigh and allocated to Salisbury for its entire working life, being withdrawn in 1964.

It was bought from Barry scrapyard by the Eastleigh Railway Preservation Society and moved to Eastleigh works on March 6, 1981, where restoration to main line condition was supervised by the late Harry H Frith, – former erecting shop foreman – by a team of volunteers.

Returned to steam in September 1992, the restoration was complete in 1993 and running-in took place on the East Somerset Railway. Main line railtours took the engine to such diverse routes as the Settle & Carlisle and the North Wales Coast line, and in 1996 the locomotive was named *Harry H Frith*.

A period of running on the Swanage Railway followed, until expiry of the boiler certificate in 2002. In 2004, the locomotive was moved to the Mid-Hants Railway for a further overhaul, which is expected to be relatively straightforward.

S15 4-6-0 No. 828 restarts its train having stalled on Honiton bank with Pathfinder Tours' 'Exe-Parrett' tour from Bristol to Exeter on October 8, 1994.

No. 30830 rests at Barry scrapyard on August 15, 1974. JOHN TITLOW

S15 4-6-0 No. 828 crosses Ais Gill viaduct on the Settle & Carlisle line with Pathfinder Tours' 'Cumbrian Mountain Express' on May 7, 1994. JOHN WHITELEY

S15 4-6-0 No. 830

No. 830 was bought by Maunsell Locomotive Society member David Jones as a source of spares for the society's No. 847 in September 1987.

All that remains though are frames, cylinders, wheelsets and a boiler, which is in poor condition.

No. 830 was moved to Sheffield Park on the Bluebell Railway on September 28, 1987, and there was once even a suggestion of converting it to a King Arthur 4-6-0, but nothing came of it. This plan has been dropped, but No. 830 was purchased by the society in 1996, but it was then decided that restoration was way beyond

the available resources and it was sold, the proceeds being allocated to the purchase of Schools class 4-4-0 No. 928 *Stowe*.

No. 830 was purchased by the Essex Locomotive Group and what remains is on the North Yorkshire Moors Railway. A condition of sale is that the locomotive will be restored as No. 830, but in the meantime the Group's S15 No. 825 has donated its frames to its No. 841 after the latter's several years' service, so No. 825 is now the operational one. It is envisaged that the rest of No. 841 can act as an eventual source of spares for No. 830, but restoration has not yet begun.

S15 4-6-0 No. 841 at Darlington after the Rail 150 cavalcade from Shildon on August 31, 1975.

S15 4-6-0 No. 841 *Greene King*

No. 30841 was a relatively early purchase from Barry scrapyard, and therefore fairly complete and in reasonable condition. Moved by the Essex Locomotive Group to the Stour Valley Railway at Chappell & Wakes Colne on September 23, 1972, the engine returned to steam in 1974, in SR livery, carrying the name *Greene King*, a local brewery which had sponsored the restoration.

The Stour Valley branch never closed as expected so the site never developed into a full scale railway, later becoming the East Anglian Railway Museum, but its track was slewed in August 1975 to connect with the BR branch, so that No. 841 could travel under its own steam to the Stockton & Darlington Railway 150th anniversary celebrations at Shildon, Co. Durham, taking part in the cavalcade on August 31, 1975.

With a main line certificate, it was agreed that a suitable route for main line operations could be found in East Anglia, Manningtree to Ely being settled on, with turning facilities

S15 4-6-0 No. 841 passes Ely North Junction with a railtour from Manningtree on September 18, 1976.

either end. In the event, No. 841 ran beyond Ely on April 3, 1976, but failed on arrival at March. A second run in September saw No. 841 set out on its return journey but still did not complete it satisfactorily.

A third run on the same route in October 1977, saw a disastrous valve gear failure on the Great Eastern main line approaching Ipswich and No. 841's main line career was over.

It was towed to the Nene Valley Railway, quickly repaired and worked trains on the recently reopened line until its owning group decided to relocate to the North Yorkshire Moors Railway, where it arrived under its own steam on December 9, 1978.

A useful member of the operating fleet for many years, it was found to have twisted frames and these were replaced by those from No. 825, the hybrid engine taking the identity of the latter. No. 841 is likely to donate further parts to the eventual restoration of No. 830.

S15 4-6-0 No. 841 and DB 2-6-2T No. 64305 at Wansford on the Nene Valley Railway on March 26, 1978.

The sad remains of No. 841 at Grosmont.

In SR black livery, No. 841 climbs the 1-in-49 past Darnholm on the North Yorkshire Moors Railway on March 29, 1991.

S15 4-6-0 No. 847

No. 847 was the last S15 to be built and was completed in December 1936. It was first allocated to Exmouth Junction, one of the biggest sheds on the Southern. No. 30847 was saved from Barry scrapyard by the 847 Locomotive Preservation Fund, moving to the Bluebell Railway in October 1978, where the 847 team soon merged with the Maunsell Locomotive Society.

Restoration of the locomotive however did not commence until 1983 as other projects were under way, and it took 10 years to complete the job. The boiler was in good condition, the existing BR tubes seeing further service, but the cylinders needed liners, and a full motion set had to be acquired. Its tender was from No. 828.

When No. 847 entered service on November 13, 1992, it quickly became a regular performer. However, its boiler had been hydraulically tested in 1988, since which the rules of certification were changed and this date became the start date for the 10 year boiler certificate. No. 847's first period of service was short therefore and it was withdrawn for overhaul after only five years. The overhaul was completed and the engine re-entered traffic at Christmas 2013.

No. 847 back in steam on December 29, 2013, after its second overhaul on the Bluebell Railway.
NICK GILLIAM

N15 King Arthur class 4-6-0
No. 777 *Sir Lamiel*

The N15 King Arthur class 4-6-0 was introduced by Robert Urie on the LSWR in 1918 for express services from Waterloo to the West Country, with names associated with the area and the legend of King Arthur and the Knights of the Round Table. Sir Lamiel of Cardiff was one of these knights and said to be a 'great lover'.

After steaming problems, the SR chief mechanical engineer Richard Maunsell made modifications in 1925 including a modified chimney and changes to the blastpipe, which improved performance, and the class eventually totalled 81 locomotives.

No. 777 *Sir Lamiel* was one of a batch of 30 built by North British for the SR in 1925. These engines had a narrower cab for use on the Eastern Section of the SR and had 5000 gallon bogie tenders. Smoke deflectors were fitted in December 1927.

Originally E777, it was first allocated to Nine Elms, but later worked from Battersea, Bournemouth, Dover, Feltham and Basingstoke. *Sir Lamiel* was withdrawn from service in October 1961 after a relatively short working life of 36 years.

After withdrawal, *Sir Lamiel* was first stored at Fratton along with other Southern locomotives earmarked for the National Collection; then Stratford from September 21, 1964, and Preston Park from March 1968. Placed on loan to the Standard Gauge Steam Trust at Tyseley and arriving on September 7, 1970, the unrestored engine was on view to the public at occasional open days but moved to a more appropriate home at the South Eastern Steam Centre at Ashford in 1973.

LEFT: In snowy conditions and while based at Hull, King Arthur class 4-6-0 No. 777 *Sir Lamiel* passes Bell Busk with a 'Cumbrian Mountain Express' to Carlisle on December 27, 1984.

Running without smoke deflectors, No. 777 *Sir Lamiel* tops Ais Gill summit with a 'Cumbrian Mountain Express' on May 26, 1990.

The centre at Ashford closed and the omens for the engine started to look much better when it was placed on loan by the National Railway Museum to the Humberside Locomotive Preservation Group, arriving at its base at Dairycoates shed in Hull on June 28, 1977. Restoration to main line standards took place there under the supervision of chief engineer Tom Tighe and the first steaming in preservation took place on February 21, 1982, restored to SR olive green livery.

On March 27 that year, it took its first main line trip over the famous Settle and Carlisle line, with the precaution of an LMS 'Black Five' as backup. Its main line career has seen the engine visit many parts of the country, returning to the Southern Region in June 1992. It spent a period based at Marylebone, working dining trains to Stratford-upon-Avon.

Following a second overhaul in preservation in 1989, its main line career continued, now more often working in Southern territory, and now in BR Brunswick green livery, and it moved to the Great Central Railway on October 4, 1995, where a further overhaul took place. A further period of running on the main line and heritage lines followed.

Following repair work at Tyseley and Loughborough, in October 2012, *Sir Lamiel* emerged in SR malachite green livery. It remains in the custody of the 5305 Locomotive Association, the successor to the Humberside Locomotive Preservation Group, and runs regularly on the Great Central Railway with visits to other railways.

Although intended for further main line work, it was increasingly found to be out of gauge, particularly on the SR routes it had always been associated with, and a decision was made in 2013 to withdraw it from the main line, with the locomotive spending the summer under repair on the North Norfolk Railway before returning to work on the Great Central..

Now in BR Brunswick green livery, No. 30777 *Sir Lamiel* passes Vauxhall.
WARWICK FALCONER

ABOVE: N15 King Arthur class 4-6-0 No. 30777 *Sir Lamiel* approaches Bincombe Tunnel on the climb of Upwey bank out of Weymouth.
WARWICK FALCONER

LEFT: Returning to the main line after a second overhaul, this time at Loughborough, No. 30777 *Sir Lamiel* passes Whitacre east of Birmingham with a Vintage Trains' Tyseley - York excursion on July 8, 2006.

N class 2-6-0 No. 31874 departs from Ropley in the first year of operations on the Mid-Hants Railway on July 3, 1977.

N class 2-6-0

The N class 2-6-0 was introduced by the SECR in 1917, the first type to be designed by Richard Maunsell for mixed-traffic duties. It was the first non-GWR locomotive class to follow the basic design principles established by George Jackson Churchward, based on his 4300 class, with Midland Railway features brought in by Maunsell's chief locomotive draughtsman, James Clayton.

With the help of former GWR engineer Harold Holcroft, it influenced future 2-6-0 development in Britain and was mechanically similar to the K class 2-6-4T.

Some 80 N class locomotives were built in three batches between the two world wars. 50 were assembled from parts made at the Royal Arsenal, Woolwich, giving rise to the nickname of 'Woolworths'. The SECR was known for the poor quality of its track and its weak, lightly built bridges.

On former LCDR sections, flint beach pebbles laid down on a bed of ash had been used for ballast but this was not as effective as normal ballast and failed to prevent track movement under strain.

In SR days, Maunsell carried out comparative trials between his N class moguls and other designs inherited by the SR. Although the LSWR S15 4-6-0 was superior in freight haulage capacity and operational economy, the N class was adopted as the company's standard mixed-traffic design.

The SR bought 50 'Woolwich' kits for assembly at Ashford between June 1924 and August 1925.

The Metropolitan Railway also bought six kits for conversion to K class 2-6-4T tank engines, which were similar in outline to the SECR K class.

N class 2-6-0 No. 31874

N class 2-6-0 No. 31874 running in red livery as No. 5 James, accelerates past Woodthorpe Lane on the Great Central Railway in May 1994.

Only one member of the N class survived, No. 31874, which arrived at the Mid-Hants Railway on March 16, 1974 from Woodham's scrapyard in Barry.

One of the 'Woolwich' batch, it was steamed for the first time in preservation in 1977, and was operational at the railway's reopening in April of that year. It has carried the names Aznar Line

and Brian Fisk in preservation and in May 1985 was the first steam engine for 18 years to haul a train into Alton.

The Mid-Hants Railway made its Thomas the Tank Engine events particularly popular and expanded its range of Thomas characters, even turning No. 31874 out in red livery as No. 5 James from 1993 for a few years, during which time it visited other railways in this guise. However it was withdrawn in 1998 due to problems that will require firebox reconstruction, and is still stored pending heavy overhaul.

In SR black livery, No. 1874 in store awaiting overhaul at Ropley on the Mid-Hants Railway in July 2013.

U class 2-6-0

Visually very similar to the N class, the U class 2-6-0s were designed by Richard Maunsell after his appointment as CME of the SR and were designed primarily for passenger use, having larger wheels. As a development of Maunsells N class 2-6-0 and K class 2-6-4T for the SECR, they originally derived from Churchward's 4300 class mogul on the GWR.

In fact the first 20 members of the U class were rebuilds of the K class 2-6-4Ts, one of which was involved in a serious derailment at Sevenoaks. A further 20 were built in 1928 which had originally been ordered as K class engines while a further batch of 10 followed, giving a total of 50 locomotives.

The K class tank engines were the passenger counterpart to the N class 2-6-0 mixed-traffic design, and were noted for rough-riding over the cheaply laid track of the former SECR. The class was withdrawn from service, and the inquiry that followed determined that the rough-riding contributed to the crash. Its recommendation was that the K class should be rebuilt to 2-6-0 tender locomotives,

The first rebuild was A805 *River Camel*, which became the first U class locomotive in service in March 1928, three months before the first production locomotive under construction at Brighton.

The U class was a reliable and economical design more than capable of attaining speeds in excess of 70mph. They were distributed more widely than their N class counterparts, although the Us were out of gauge for the Tonbridge-Hastings line.

Withdrawals took place between 1962 and 1966, by which time the class was concentrated around Guildford.

Contrasting shades of Southern green as SR U class 2-6-0 No. 1618 and West Country Pacific No. 21C123 *Blackmore Vale* climb Freshfield bank on the Bluebell Railway on May 13, 1979.

U class 2-6-0 No. 1618

No. 1618 was one of the class originally ordered as a K class 2-6-4T, but when outshopped from Brighton in October 1928 as a 2-6-0, it was allocated to Guildford shed.

For the next 17 years it worked on the North Downs line from Reading to Redhill and between Eastleigh and Woking. A few alterations were made such as smoke deflectors fitted in 1935. From December 1945 it was moved to a Salisbury sub-shed at Andover to work the SR line to Swindon. At Nationalisation in 1948 it was reallocated again to Nine Elms and moved around until settling for a while at Eastleigh in 1954 to work the Hampshire routes.

Two years later it moved again, to Basingstoke and the final transfer came later in 1963, back to its original shed at Guildford. In January 1964 it steamed for the last time, having covered 1,143,942 miles in 1935 and was sold for scrap to Woodham's scrapyard. No. 1618 was only the second engine to leave Barry scrapyard, on January 19, 1969.

At first it was moved to a siding at New Hythe cement works in Kent, where members of the Southern Mogul Preservation Society spent two and a half years trying to restore the engine in basic conditions. The Kent and East Sussex Railway at Tenterden had just received its Light Railway Order and the society was able to complete the job after moving the locomotive to Tenterden in October 1972.

However, the track on the KESR was not built to take the weight of such a locomotive and when No. 1618 was steamed in May 1974, all that could be done was demonstration shunting in Tenterden station.

On May 17, 1977 three years after the first steaming, the society which was to change its name to the Maunsell Locomotive Society, moved its engine to the Bluebell Railway, a move which was highly successful. It saw out its 10-year boiler certificate and was given another general overhaul almost immediately. Since expiry of its second 10-year certificate though, it has been on display in Sheffield Park shed, while the overhaul of a second U class, No. 1638 was in progress.

In BR black livery, No. 31618 stands at Sheffield Park on July 7, 2013.

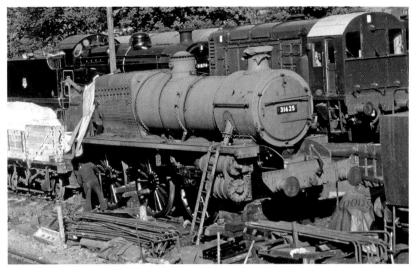

U class 2-6-0 No. 31625
under restoration at Ropley
on the Mid-Hants Railway on
June 14, 1987.

U class No. 31625

No. 31625 arrived on the Mid-Hants Railway from Barry scrapyard in March 1980.

Returned to steam in September 1996, it worked its first revenue-earning train on the MHR on 14th and completed a main line test run on February 20, 1997. After a number of false starts it finally took its place at the head of a main line railtour on September 13, 1997, from Waterloo to Bristol, the first railtour to be operated by the Mid-Hants Railway. It enjoyed a short period of main line operation and even participated in London Transport's Steam On The Met event in 1999, but when N class No. 31874 was withdrawn from service, No. 31625 took over as the Thomas the Tank Engine character *James*, running in red livery as No. 5 until withdrawal from use.

RIGHT: In faded red livery,
No. 31625 is dumped out of
use at Ropley on the Mid-
Hants Railway in July 2013.

U class 2-6-0 No. 1638
departs from Horsted
Keynes on the
Bluebell Railway.

U class 2-6-0 No. 1638

Having returned No. 1618 to traffic on the Bluebell Railway, the Maunsell Society became involved with sister engine No. 1638, the 114th engine to leave Barry. It arrived at the Bluebell Railway on July 30, 1980, purchased by Bluebell member George Nickson, and generously donated to the railway. Until 1993 though, the engine stood in Turners sidings at Sheffield Park.

When the society completed S15 4-6-0 No. 847, the options were to restore the other S15, No. 830 or take advantage of an offer from the Bluebell Railway, to take the U, No. 1638 on a free 50-year lease, provided it was restored for future use on the Bluebell. This was accepted and No. 1638's overhaul was completed. It entered service in February 2006.

U class 2-6-0 No. 31806 at Ropley on July 3, 1977 shortly after arrival from Barry scrapyard.

No. 31806 departs from Corfe Castle on the Swanage Railway during a Matt Allen/ Warwick Falconer photo charter in September 2013.
PETER ZABEK

U class 2-6-0 No. 31806

No. 31806 was an early acquisition from Barry scrapyard for service on the Mid-Hants Railway, arriving on the line in October 1976.

It returned to steam in April 1981, and became a regular engine on the line.

Unlike the other two Southern moguls, when No. 31806 was due for its 10-year overhaul this was carried out and the engine returned to traffic in February 2011.

Just as the overhaul was completed though, a serious fire in the locomotive shed at Ropley resulted in damage to No. 31806's tender and one from the Maunsell Society's No. 1618 on the Bluebell Railway was borrowed, painted BR black and attached to No. 31806 to enable it to enter service.

The mogul has been a popular visitor to other heritage lines in recent years and is expected to move away from the MHR in 2014.

Schools class 4-4-0

The SR V class 4-4-0, more commonly known as the Schools class, was designed by Richard Maunsell for the SR, being a smaller version of his Lord Nelson 4-6-0 but also incorporating components from Urie and Maunsell's N15 King Arthur 4-6-0. With three cylinders and well-liked by crews, it was the last 4-4-0 to be designed in Britain and was the most powerful class of this wheel arrangement ever produced in Europe, having a higher tractive effort than the nominally more powerful King Arthurs.

All 40 were named after English public schools, and were designed to provide a powerful class of intermediate express passenger locomotive for lines which could cope with high-axle loads but had short turntables. Some of the best performances by the class were on the heavily restricted Tonbridge to Hastings line.

At first, the locomotives worked on the Central and Eastern Sections but after the electrification of the London to Eastbourne and the London to Portsmouth routes in the late 1930s, 10 of the class were transferred for use on the Bournemouth line. They operated until 1961 when mass withdrawals took place and all had gone by December 1962.

ABOVE: Schools class 4-4-0 No. 30925 *Cheltenham* in unrestored condition at the Dinting Railway Centre in Derbyshire on June 20, 1976.

BELOW: SR Schools class 4-4-0 No. 925 *Cheltenham* passes Chawton on the Mid-Hants Railway on January 27, 2013. WARWICK FALCONER

Schools class 4-4-0 No. 925 *Cheltenham*

Having been nominated for preservation as part of the National Collection, No. 30925 *Cheltenham* was initially stored at Fratton until relocated to Stratford on September 21, 1964 and Preston Park on February 19, 1968. It was loaned for occasional display at Tyseley arriving on September 7, 1970, but when moved to the Dinting Railway Centre at Glossop on January 30, 1973, it was still in unrestored condition.

After moving to York in November 1977 it was quickly put back in steam and appeared in the Rocket 150 cavalcade at Rainhill in May 1980 commemorating the 150th anniversary of the opening of the Liverpool & Manchester Railway, travelling to and from the event under its own steam, and on to the National Railway Museum at York from Dinting in November 1977. It never hauled a train during this period though and took its place in the museum as a static exhibit.

It was eventually overhauled by a team from the Mid-Hants Railway led by Chris Smith at Eastleigh Works. On completion, it featured at the NRM's Railfest at York in June 2012 and then returned to the Mid-Hants on June 28 to take its place in the railway's operating fleet, while making regular visits to other railways.

No. 925 *Cheltenham* crosses the reinstated embankment at Chicken Curve near Winchcombe, returning to Toddington at the Gloucestershire Warwickshire Railway's Cotswold Steam Celebration gala on May 25, 2013. PAUL STRATFORD

Schools class 4-4-0 No. 925 *Cheltenham* in the Rocket 150 cavalcade at Rainhill on May 25, 1980.

Paul Kirkman officially relaunches *Cheltenham,* a year after it returned to steam. ROBIN JONES

Schools class 4-4-0 No. 30926 *Repton*

No. 30926 *Repton* was built at Eastleigh in May 1934, and entered service on the Bournemouth route, with some time operating between Waterloo and Portsmouth before that line was electrified. It was one of the last of the class to be overhauled by BR in 1960, so was considered a good choice for preservation after withdrawal in December 1962. After a period of storage, it returned to Eastleigh Works in April 1966 and was externally restored and outshopped on February 28, 1967, being shipped to Montreal on *SS Roonah Head* from Gladstone Dock, Liverpool in April 1967.

It was displayed at the Steamtown museum at Bellows Falls, Vermont from November 1967 and was loaned to the Cape Breton Steam Railway in Canada for a period of operation, but it become somewhat uncared for by the museum. It was repatriated to the UK, arriving at Brightlingsea on April 10, 1989. Back in the UK, the engine was restored before quickly moving on to the North Yorkshire Moors Railway where it was used regularly before being loaned to the Great Central Railway from 1991 to 1993.

Back on the NYMR, it became the first Schools to operate on the main line since 1962 when it was upgraded to haul trains on the Esk Valley line between Whitby and Battersby. It is currently awaiting overhaul.

ABOVE: Soon after its return to service, Schools class 4-4-0 No. 30926 *Repton* climbs the 1-in-49 grade at Beck Hole on March 29, 1991.

RIGHT: Schools class 4-4-0 No. 30926 *Repton* on the Great Central Railway approaching Leicester North on November 9, 1991.

BELOW RIGHT: A Schools on the main line; No. 30926 *Repton* departs from Whitby.

BELOW: No. 30926 *Repton* climbs past Darnholm on the North Yorkshire Moors Railway on December 30, 2003.

RIGHT: No. 928 *Stowe* on display at the Montagu Motor Museum at Beaulieu in Hampshire. JEFF COLLEDGE

Schools class 4-4-0 No. 928 *Stowe*

No. 928 *Stowe* was built in 1934 at Eastleigh and recorded more than a million miles of passenger service operation, achieving the fastest recorded speed for the class of 95mph, near Wool in 1938 on a four-coach train.

Stowe was transferred to its last shed at Brighton in November 1961 and withdrawn a year later on November 17, 1962.

It was purchased by Lord Montagu for his National Motor Museum at Beaulieu in Hampshire and displayed in the open with three 'Bournemouth Belle' Pullman cars from February 14, 1964, though this was a train *Stowe* never appears to have hauled.

On February 2, 1973 though, it was moved by road to Eastleigh Works, where it joined David Shepherd's two BR Standards Nos. 92203 and 75029 which had been rendered homeless by the collapse of the Longmoor steam centre. It was towed on November 18, 1973 as part of two convoys of locomotives and stock headed by David Shepherd's engines, to Cranmore where the East Somerset Railway was to be established.

July 17, 1980 saw an unrepeatable opportunity for *Stowe* to be purchased by the Maunsell Locomotive Society, and it was moved to the Bluebell Railway to be put into running order, returning to steam in June 1981.

The engine was withdrawn on expiry of its 10-year certificate and remains on static display at Sheffield Park.

ABOVE: Schools class 4-4-0 No. 928 *Stowe* passes Holywell on the Bluebell Railway on June 14, 1981.

LEFT: Schools class 4-4-0 No. 928 *Stowe* at Horsted Keynes on June 14, 1981.

ABOVE: Lord Nelson 4-6-0 No. 30850 *Lord Nelson* at Church Fenton en route from York to Carnforth for restoration, hauled by LNER A3 Pacific No. 4472 *Flying Scotsman* on December 3, 1977.

FAR RIGHT: SR 4-6-0 No. 850 *Lord Nelson* tackles the 1-in-50 of Upwey bank out of Weymouth with Kingfisher Tours' 'Dorset Coast Express' on May 19, 2007. DAVID HOLMAN

Lord Nelson 4-6-0 No. 850 *Lord Nelson*

E850 was the first of the Lord Nelson or LN class 4-6-0s, entering service in August 1926, of which only 16 were built. This was Maunsell's first completely new design for the SR, in response to requirements for a locomotive to be able to handle 500 tonne Continental expresses from the Channel ports.

The Nelsons were among the biggest locomotives in Britain and unique in having their crank axles set at 135°, to give eight softer 'puffs' per revolution of the driving wheels rather than four heavy ones and therefore produced a more even pull on the fire.

Unfortunately, within a couple of years, the class acquired a reputation for poor steaming and many firemen were unable to master firing the long, narrow firebox.

However, experience and modifications produced such times as 80-81 minutes from Southampton to Waterloo and similar times from Salisbury, with up to 14 coaches, which at last showed what a Nelson could do.

From 1940 their lives were spent on the Western Section, but by the 1950s they had been displaced by the Bulleid Pacifics.

No. 30850 itself was withdrawn in August 1962 and selected for official preservation, taking up residence initially at Fratton, along with other SR locomotives, moving to Stratford on September 13, 1964 and Preston Park on February 12, 1967.

It remained there until 1977, when it was moved to the NRM at York but was quickly transferred on to Carnforth, being hauled there by *Flying Scotsman* on December 3 that year.

RIGHT: No. 30850 on arrival at Carnforth for restoration to working order on December 3, 1977.

OPPOSITE RIGHT: On its first main line run in preservation, No. 850 *Lord Nelson* passes Whitbeck on a Carnforth-Sellafield 'Cumbrian Coast Express' on August 25, 1980.

SR 4-6-0 No. 850 *Lord Nelson* departs from Waterloo with Steam Dreams' 'Southern Sunset' on July 8, 2007, which terminated at Westbury after the locomotive failed.
JOHN TITLOW

Like many locomotives withdrawn in the 1960s, *Lord Nelson* was still in reasonable condition being surplus rather than 'worn out'. Restoration to working order commenced at Carnforth and was completed just in time for an appearance at the Rocket 150 cavalcade at Rainhill in May 1980.

This was followed by a series of successful railtours taking in the Settle & Carlisle and the Cumbrian Coast routes, where No. 850 impressed with its power and reliability. Unfortunately, firebox problems led to early withdrawal and a further period of storage as a static exhibit at Carnforth.

It was known that the engine's boiler was probably at the end of its useful life and it was looking for a new home, which is where the Eastleigh Railway Preservation Society came in. Negotiations

with the National Railway Museum at York were successful and *Lord Nelson* returned south on August 30, 1997, thirty-five years since last being seen at Eastleigh. A further return to active service depended on a successful Heritage Lottery Fund application, as the boiler required extremely heavy repairs or even total replacement. The engine was eventually returned to steam and undertook a main line test run from Carnforth conducted by West Coast Railways on March 7, 2007.

A few railtours took place on the Southern Region but major boiler problems were still encountered and *Lord Nelson* found itself sidelined on the Mid-Hants Railway. It proved possible to effect repairs to enable it to continue to run there, but any full-scale return to the main line looks a long way off.

SR 4-6-0 No. 850 *Lord Nelson* passes Chawton with a goods train on the Mid-Hants Railway on March 25, 2012. WARWICK FALCONER

Q class 0-6-0 No. 541

The Q class 0-6-0 was Maunsell's last design for the SR, but suffered from poor steaming, which was cured by Bulleid, who had taken over as CME by the time the engines entered service, by fitting a wide-bore Lemaître chimney and multiple jet blastpipe, which did not help the engine's appearance

No. 541 was allocated to Guildford when new in January 1939, and worked mainly on pick-up goods trains but also some passenger workings on the North Downs line. It even had a near miss from a Second World War bomb at Betchworth, although not directly hit, it was derailed and the damage repairs can still be seen on the boiler and firebox.

The 20 Qs were quite quickly displaced by Bulleid's own 0-6-0 design, the more powerful Q1.

After moving around the area, 1953 took No. 30541 to Bournemouth shed for 10 years, being associated with the Lymington and Swanage branches. Busy summer months especially would bring passenger work in this area, but the final couple of years were spent back at Guildford from where it was withdrawn in November 1964, becoming the only engine of its class to find its way to Barry scrapyard.

No. 541 was bought for £3250 in 1973 by the Southern Q Fund and moved to the Dowty Railway Centre at Ashchurch in Gloucestershire on May 15, 1974, the 54th loco to leave Woodhams. The site had to be vacated in 1977, however, so the Maunsell Q Locomotive Preservation Society moved it to the Bluebell Railway on October 5, 1978, and after a short time the Q Group and the Maunsell Locomotive Society, as it now was, merged to pool their resources.

By July 1980 the boiler was back in place, a year later the cab was on, and by 1983 all fittings were in place and it was steamed for the first time in 19 years.

From the outset, No. 541 was a success at the Bluebell and consistently had the highest annual mileage of all steamable locomotives until its ticket expired in 1993. A return to steam after overhaul is eagerly anticipated.

No. 541 passes under Three Arch Bridge on December 31, 1989. JOHN TITLOW

The frames of No. 541 at Sheffield Park on July 7, 2013.

USA class 0-6-0T

The SR USA class was made up of 15 of an original 382 ex-US Army Corps of Engineers' S100 0-6-0Ts built between 1942 and 1944 and intended to support the US war effort in Europe before and after D-Day. After the war, survivors were employed in a number of countries including France, Austria, Greece, Egypt, Palestine, Iraq and Yugoslavia.

Originally 42 members of the type had been loaned to the War Department in 1943 and placed in storage at Newbury Racecourse station. 15 of these were purchased by the Southern Railway, for £2500 each, with 14 being put to use at Southampton docks, replacing a variety of older engines. Others found industrial uses with the National Coal Board, Longmoor Military

Railway and Austin Motors. The key to their success was their short wheelbase, which was able to negotiate the tight curves found at Southampton docks. They were also powerful, able to haul heavy freight trains as well as passenger trains in the docks.

The SR's locomotives were built in 1942 either at the Vulcan Iron Works in Wilkes-Barre, Pennsylvania or HK Porter Inc of Pittsburgh.

Of the 42 WD USA tanks, nine remained in use by the military or the NCB in the 1960s, and five of the BR ones survived until the end of steam on the SR in 1967, having been transferred to departmental use at workshops and locomotive sheds.

USA class 0-6-0T No. 65

In 1963, USA 0-6-0Ts Nos. 30065 (originally WD No. 1968) and 30070, now surplus to requirements at Southampton docks, were transferred to departmental stock, renumbered DS237 and DS238 respectively and sent to Ashford Wagon Works. No. 30065 was painted malachite green and named *Maunsell* after the Southern Railway's first chief mechanical engineer.

The pair were kept busy at Ashford until April 1967 when DS237 was laid aside, to be followed two months later by DS238. In March 1968 they were sold to Woodham's scrapyard at Barry in South Wales but, predictably, ran hot while under tow and did not get further than Tonbridge. There they remained on the site of the former locomotive shed until resold to the Kent & East Sussex Railway in August 1968, arriving at Rolvenden on September 7.

In accordance with its independent Col Stephens' tradition, the KESR initially adopted its own livery and numbering system

for the two locomotives; DS237 became KESR No. 22, while DS238 became No. 21. KESR No. 22 became the first large locomotive to enter service on the reopened, now heritage, line, in 1974, proving itself very capable of hauling five coach trains up Tenterden bank. It had been fitted with an extended coal bunker and improved lubrication to overcome its bearing problems. In 1978 it exchanged boilers with No. 21 re-entered service in April 1981 after overhaul in black livery, but was taken out of traffic at the end of the 1990 season.

After another heavy overhaul, the locomotive re-entered service as Southern Railway No. 65 in the summer of 1997 in its original postwar livery of black with sunshine lettering. After 2002, a new firebox was fitted and after a further overhaul, the engine returned to service in 2008.

In 2012, No. 65 went on loan to the Embsay & Bolton Abbey Railway in West Yorkshire, returning to the KESR in 2013.

USA class 0-6-0T No. 65 on Tenterden bank on the Kent & East Sussex Railway.

USA class 0-6-0T No. 65 at Bolton Abbey on the Embsay & Bolton Abbey Steam Railway on December 9, 2012.

USA class 0-6-0T No. 70

WD No. 1960 was put into service by the SR in April 1947 as No. 70, becoming No. 30070 after Nationalisation.

In August 1963, the engine was transferred to departmental stock at Ashford Wagon Works, painted malachite green, renumbered DS238 and named *Wainwright* after the SECR's first locomotive superintendent.

DS238 was finally retired in June 1967 just before the end of SR steam. With DS237, it was sold to Woodham's scrapyard but, as with DS237, was resold to the KESR in August 1968, arriving at Rolvenden on September 6. DS238 became KESR No. 21

Unlike its sister, DS238 spent many years out of use, its boiler having been exchanged with its sister. Restoration work only commenced in 1988, the engine entering traffic in 1994 as DS238 *Wainwright,* in correct malachite green livery.

Extensive modifications had been made to the cab and bunker. The KESR's two USA tanks were finally seen in steam together on the line over the weekend of July 26-27 1997. After taking part in the 150th anniversary of railways at the National Railway Museum in York in 2004, DS238 was withdrawn for overhaul.

USA 0-6-0T DS 238 on display at the National Railway Museum's Railfest event in 2004. FRED KERR

USA class 0-6-0T No. 30064 accelerates away from Sheffield Park on the Bluebell Railway on June 27, 1976.

USA class 0-6-0T No. 30064

No. 30064 ended its BR days as an Eastleigh works shunter, and on withdrawal in 1967 was sold to the Southern Loco Preservation Co. Ltd, and was preserved on the Meon Valley Railway at Droxford, Hampshire in 1968, being steamed there in September that year.

After the Droxford scheme came to nothing, it moved after a period of storage at Fareham, to the Longmoor Military Railway on May 30, 1970. Though little used, it did play a starring role in the 1972 feature film *Young Winston*.

Following the collapse of the Longmoor steam centre, No. 30064 with the other SLP stock, was moved to the Bluebell Railway that now owns it. It arrived on October 24, 1971 and following a number of years in use, it now awaits major boiler work, and is a likely volunteer restoration project for a few years' time.

In 2003 it was repainted into wartime livery as WD 1959.

In orange livery, USA class 0-6-0T No. 72 and LMS 'Black Five' 4-6-0 No. 45212 head away from Ingrow on the Keighley & Worth Valley Railway on March 27, 1977.

USA class 0-6-0T No. 30072

No. 30072, one-time Guildford shed pilot was purchased by Rochdale solicitor Richard Greenwood and moved to the Keighley & Worth Valley Railway in Yorkshire on January 14, 1968. It was quickly steamed and played its part in the railway's reopening ceremony on June 30 that year just before the end of BR steam. It carried an orange livery based on the Southern Pacific GS4 'Daylight' 4-8-4 locomotives, but in more recent years has reverted to its BR identity in malachite green.

Back in BR malachite green, USA class 0-6-0T No. 30072 climbs away from Keighley on January 29, 1980.

USA class 0-6-0T No. 30075

The number of preserved USA tanks was augmented by two ex-Jugoslavian Railways Class 62 locomotives, built to a broadly similar design, which were imported to be converted to British USA class specifications.

The first of these, JZ No. 62.669, built in 1960, arrived on the Swanage Railway on December 15, 1990, having been bought by a group of SR members.

The restoration team led by Martyn Ashworth returned the engine to steam on December 19, 1991, with a return to service in August 1992.

It has since worked on the East Somerset Railway and spent some time at Barrow Hill Roundhouse in Derbyshire, although a further overhaul is now approaching completion on the Great Central Railway (Nottingham) at Ruddington.

USA class 0-6-0T No. 30075 departs from Corfe Castle on the Swanage Railway on July 8, 2007.

A second imported USA tank lookalike arrived on the Mid-Hants Railway from Bosnia on December 11 2006. It had always been the intention of the owners of No. 30075, Project 62 Locomotive Group, to obtain a second engine and the plan is to make it 'disabled-friendly' by rebuilding the cab to enable disabled access.

Many locomotives of the type were built in Yugoslavia in the 1950s and around 45 were thought to exist in Eastern Europe along with about ten genuine examples.

It had been overhauled in 1989 and worked until 2004, when it was withdrawn and a further overhaul had commenced at Mittal Steel Zenicam at Zenica. Obtaining the second engine was inevitably delayed by the Balkan conflict, but negotiations to purchase it were facilitated by the commercial department of the British Embassy in Sarajevo.

ABOVE: No. 30075 is the only steam locomotive of a design used by the Southern Railway which has seen service on regular timetabled services on the Dartmoor Railway which runs from Okehampton to Meldon Quarry on the one time LSWR 'Withered Arm' main line to Plymouth. ROBIN JONES

LEFT: No. 62.521 at Zenica being prepared for its journey on December 8 2006 PROJECT 62

CHAPTER 9

OVS Bulleid

Bulleid was unique among steam engineers; his wartime designs were unorthodox, yet he is remembered for one of the finest express steam locomotive designs ever to run in Britain.

Oliver Vaughan Snell (OVS) Bulleid took over from Maunsell as chief mechanical engineer of the Southern Railway in 1937, having been a protege of Nigel Gresley on the London & North Eastern Railway, particularly involved in some of Gresley's more unconventional design thinking. He inherited Maunsell's Q class 0-6-0 and oversaw completion of the order. He was to transform the SR motive power scene in a way that would have been undreamed of at the time.

Bulleid was born in New Zealand in 1882 but moved when his mother returned to Wales in 1889. He joined the Great Northern Railway on January 21, 1901 as a premium apprentice at Doncaster works under HA Ivatt.

Moving through the ranks, Bulleid was promoted to works manager and chief draughtsman in 1908, also marrying Ivatt's youngest daughter in that year.

After two years working for the Board of Trade he returned to the GNR as Nigel Gresley's personal assistant in 1912.

In LNER days, he was heavily involved in Gresley's P2 2-8-2 and high speed exploits by *Flying Scotsman* and *Silver Link*.

His first contact with the Southern Railway was as an observer during investigations into the problems with the River class 2-6-4Ts after the Sevenoaks derailment in 1927.

On September 20, 1937, Bulleid joined the Southern Railway and was appointed CME on October 1, aged 54. Among his first projects were modifications to existing designs, including Lemaitre blastpipes for the Lord Nelsons and Schools and new cylinders for the Lord Nelsons. An early project to build new 2-8-2s for express work was stillborn but Bulleid pressed on with a Pacific design.

The LMS had abandoned building 0-6-0s for goods traffic when the last of the 4Fs was completed, while the GWR had built the 2251 class 0-6-0s but these were long overdue replacements for the Dean Goods 0-6-0s. The LNER though had continued to invest in 0-6-0s in a big way, the J39 being Gresley's most numerous design. So it was not altogether surprising that Bulleid was a believer in 0-6-0s for goods work and one of his new designs for the SR was the Q1, the most powerful 0-6-0 to run in Britain, and one of the most unconventional.

The first Merchant Navy Pacific emerged from Eastleigh in February 1941, the Q1 0-6-0 in 1942 and the first West Country light Pacific in June 1945. Bulleid's only other steam design was the controversial and unsuccessful Leader in 1949.

Having responsibility for coaching stock, including electric multiple units, Bulleid was involved in the SR's first diesel shunters, and main line diesel and electric locomotives.

The GWR and LMS dabbled with modern traction just before Nationalisation, and even Gresley had seriously considered diesel traction before he designed his streamlined A4 Pacifics. It was the LNER though that went for full-scale electrification of an inter-city main line as opposed to suburban services when it commenced the electrification of the Manchester – Sheffield line over Woodhead.

But it was a diehard steam man, Robert Riddles, who was appointed the CME of the newly-formed British Railways in 1948, and introduced his BR Standard classes, largely following LMS practice. With hindsight, modern traction should perhaps have been pursued a little more vigorously in the early 1950s. Bulleid's diesels were good engines and stood the test of time, essentially being developed into the English-Electric Type 4, which as the Class 40 lasted into the 1990s.

Bulleid joined CIE, the Irish Railways as CME in 1951 and died in 1970 at the age of 87.

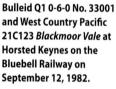

Bulleid Q1 0-6-0 No. 33001 and West Country Pacific 21C123 *Blackmoor Vale* at Horsted Keynes on the Bluebell Railway on September 12, 1982.

Q1 0-6-0 No. 33001

The Q1 0-6-0 was designed by Oliver Bulleid for use on the intensive freight workings experienced during wartime on the SR network, a total of 40 being built from 1942. Bulleid incorporated many innovations and weight-saving concepts to produce a highly functional design which lasted in service until July 1966. It was the ultimate development of the British 0-6-0 freight engine, capable of hauling heavy trains and were often known as 'Charlies'.

Using the minimum amount of raw materials, and with all superfluous features stripped away, it was the most powerful 0-6-0 steam locomotive ever to run on Britain's railways. The Q1s were light though, weighing less than 90 tons so could be used over more than 97% of the SR's route mileage.

The unusual shape was also dictated as the boiler lagging was made of a material known as 'idaglass', which, although cheap and plentiful during the war years, could not support any weight, and therefore the boiler rings had to be adapted to lend the lagging the support needed. One aspect of their shape was that, like Bulleid's SR Pacifics, they could be simply

driven through a coach washing plant, saving on manpower. Bulleid introduced a continental style of locomotive identification he came across in France, working for Westinghouse Electric before the First World War, and at the Ministry of Defence Railway Operating Division during the hostilities. This was broadly the UIC classification system where 'C' refers to three coupled driving axles. The Q1s carried the identification 'C' followed by the individual number from C1 to C40.

Withdrawn towards the end of SR steam, the first of the class, No. 33001 was initially stored at Stratford works, moving to Preston Park in March 1968 where it remained in store. A loan period to the Bluebell Railway was an obvious move, enabling the locomotive to be on public view and returned to service. Arriving on the line on May 15, 1977, complete and in good condition, it was quickly returned to steam later that year.

When a heavy overhaul was due though, it was decided to put the engine on display at the National Railway Museum at York, where it arrived on May 4, 2004.

Q1 0-6-0 No. C1 heads away from Horsted Keynes towards Kingscote on the Bluebell Railway on January 3, 1993.

Q1 0-6-0 C1 in the National Railway Museum at York.
ROBIN JONES

BULLEID NUMBERING

Bulleid had served abroad for the Railway Operating Division during the First World War and became familiar with the Continental (UIC) system of locomotive numbering where a letter denoted the number of driving wheels, A being 2, B four and C 6. He introduced this to the SR with his Q1 class which were given the identities C1 – C40.

His later Pacifics had somewhat more complicated identification, starting with 21C1.

SOUTHERN

Bulleid Firth Brown (BFB) wheels designed by Oliver Bulleid and Firth Brown were a later patent – a lighter wheel was obtained by using a strengthened rim. One of its major advantages over a spoked wheel is the more uniform support provided to the tyre.

Bulleid/Firth Brown variation of the 'Boxpok' wheel.

Bulleid Pacifics

What the Southern Railway was short of by the end of the 1930s was modern mixed traffic and large express engines, those in use essentially being of pre-Grouping design, apart from the relatively few and already outdated Lord Nelsons and the fairly small Schools.

The King Arthurs were certainly quite dated and the S15 was regarded as a goods engine, not mixed traffic like Stanier's 'Black Fives' on the LMS or Collett's GWR Halls and Granges.

But while the LMS, GWR and eventually the LNER built mixed traffic 4-6-0s in considerable numbers, Bulleid moved the goalposts and filled the gaps in the SR's motive power fleet by introducing two varieties of semi-streamlined Pacifics, similar in appearance but actually quite different in dimensions.

The Merchant Navy was a big Pacific, of class 8 power in BR parlance, but was claimed to be a mixed traffic design, having 6ft 2in driving wheels. During the war was not the best time to introduce an express engine, and while 6ft 8in was the accepted norm for express service, 6ft 2in was being found to sacrifice little in terms of top speed while giving enhanced power for heavier trains, and would prove useful in coping with the heavier grades on the SR system.

Unconventional in appearance, the Bulleid Pacific was a three-cylinder design with a boiler featuring a wide firebox, but otherwise there was little evidence of Bulleid's background on the LNER.

But they were unconventional beneath their air-smoothed casings as well, with steam reverser, Bulleid chain-driven valve gear encased in an oil bath for ease of maintenance and to eliminate the hammer-blow associated with conventional locomotives, steel fireboxes with thermic siphons and an

Battle of Britain No. 34072 *257 Squadron* and West Country No. 34105 *Swanage* doublehead a Sentimental Journeys photo charter away from Swanage on March 19, 1993.

adaptation of 'Boxpok' wheels. They were good engines, but the Q1 and the Pacifics were all that Bulleid managed to produce in terms of steam designs – apart from the Leader of course.

Initially, three batches of 10 Merchant Navies were completed, the last being delivered by British Railways following Nationalisation.

The members of the class were named after shipping companies serving Southampton Docks, highlighting the SR's connections with the Continent and international travel.

Although the Merchant Navies proved fast, free running and powerful, they had their problems. The oil bath proved impossible to keep oil tight, the chains were prone to stretching and the steam reverser was a bit unpredictable. The air-smoothed casing was a barrier to easy access when things went wrong.

However, the boiler was one of the best ever designed in Britain, although rather heavy on coal, and would deliver whatever the driver demanded, as long as the fireman could keep up with it. The 110 'light' Pacifics were nominally divided into two series, the West Country and Battle of Britain classes, but differed only in terms of their names. They were far bigger than a Hall, 'Black Five' or LNER B1 4-6-0 but kept within a similar axle loading, giving them a wide range of operation.

When tested in the 1948 Locomotive Exchanges, the Bulleid engines predictably outperformed their Big Four rivals but at the expense of coal and water consumption. It was not comparing like for like. It proved little but there was nothing else the Southern Region could realistically have put up against the 4-6-0s.

THERMIC SIPHONS are heat-exchanging elements in the firebox or combustion chamber of some steam locomotive designs. Directly exposed to the radiant heat of combustion, they have a high evaporative capacity relative to their size. By arranging them near-vertically, they also have good water circulation by means of the thermosyphon effect.

The concept of a self-circulating thermic siphon began with stationary boilers and reached its peak in steam locomotive boilers, where the complexity of a siphon was justified by the need for a compact and lightweight means of increasing boiler capacity. A thermic siphon is an integral part of the boiler and is quite different from a feedwater heater, which is an external accessory.

Located in the firebox, the thermic siphon is a funnel-shaped steel fabrication that connects the bottom of the throat sheet (the front wall of the firebox) with the crown sheet (the roof of the firebox). Feed water flows upward through the siphons from the boiler barrel. By exposing the water to the heat of the firebox, thermic siphons increase thermal efficiency and help to improve water circulation in the boiler through ensuring more uniform temperatures within it. Fresh cold water introduced from the injectors is preheated by passage

The thermic siphons are clearly visible in the sectioned Merchant Navy No. 35029 *Ellerman Lines* in the National Railway Museum at York.

through the siphons before arriving at the crown sheet, the hottest part of the boiler. Bulleid was the principal advocate of thermic siphons in British steam locomotives in his Pacifics.

SR unrebuilt Bulleid West Country Pacific No. 21C123 *Blackmoor Vale* (running as *OVS Bulleid*) gets a friendly wave from the local Home Guard as it takes the 4pm from Sheffield Park past Keysford Lane during the Bluebell's Southern at War weekend on May 10, 2008. JON BOWERS

In preservation, the two Bulleid Pacifics purchased privately from BR have been joined by no less than 27 more from Barry scrapyard, plus two are in the National Collection. They are big complicated engines, expensive to restore, maintain and operate, and many were in atrocious condition when purchased from Barry. While there have been some remarkable success stories and no less than 19 have returned to steam, many have worked for one period then entered a long period of storage. The supply of active Bulleid Pacifics has sometimes outstripped demand from the heritage lines and the number of operational ones continues to reduce slightly from a peak of 10 in 1998.

The number of organisations involved has fluctuated as groups merge, disband or fall out. Many have been resold several times and there has been much exchanging of parts. Friction between restoration and operating groups and their host railways has been particularly marked in the post-preservation Bulleid Pacific story, as restoration seems to stall for years and railways see rusting hulks taking up space but which will never see gainful employment on the line.

Nevertheless a typical cross-section of Bulleid's Pacifics can be seen in operation, with three Light Pacifics currently steamable in original form and three in rebuilt form, plus two Merchant Navies, and of these a Battle of Britain, a rebuilt West Country and one of the Merchant Navies are registered for main line use.

CHAPTER 10

The original Bulleid Pacifics

In view of the decision to terminate the rebuilding programme, many Bulleid Pacifics remained in original form until withdrawal, and some survive in preservation.

West Country Pacific No. 34007 *Wadebridge*

No. 34007 *Wadebridge* is the oldest surviving West Country Pacific and fortunately remains in original condition. It was built in Brighton during 1945 as 21C107 and ventured west to Wadebridge for an official naming ceremony on October 31 of that year.

Allocated from new to Exmouth Junction, its early years were spent in the West Country until April 1951 when it moved to Nine Elms, but was withdrawn on October 7, 1965, and sold to Woodham's scrapyard at Barry Island.

Purchased from there by the Plym Valley Railway Association, it arrived in Plymouth at Bass-Charringtons' private siding on May 23, 1981, but Wadebridge (34007) Locomotive Ltd was created to act as its owning company. It moved to the PVR base at Marsh Mills but because of a lack of space, moved to the Fitzgerald Lighting factory site alongside the Bodmin & Wenford Railway at Bodmin in March 1992.

Following many years of hard work, the rolling chassis was moved to the workshops at Bodmin General on December 1, 2001, where the rebuilding was completed, with the boiler being fitted on the frames in November 2003.

On October 2, 2006, No. 34007 *Wadebridge* made a short trip under its own steam and hauled a special train on Sunday, October 29, 2006, with a renaming ceremony at Bodmin General

performed jointly by the mayors of Bodmin and Wadebridge, Cllr Lance Kennedy and Cllr Nick Saunders.

Regular operation at Bodmin was impossible though and the engine moved to the Mid-Hants Railway, initially on a one year hire agreement.

In August 2008 the Bodmin and Wenford Railway Trust sold its 73% majority stake in the company to the Mid-Hants Railway. The engine will remain a regular performer on the line but has made visits to other railways, including the Severn Valley.

No. 34007 *Wadebridge* heads its first timetabled passenger train for 41 years, the 3.40pm from Bodmin Parkway on October 29, 2006. BERNARD MILLS

LEFT: At its permanent home, West Country Pacific No. 34007 *Wadebridge* climbs towards Medstead & Four Marks on the Mid-Hants Railway on July 7, 2007, during the lines gala to commemorate the 40th anniversary of the end of Southern steam.

BELOW: Visiting the Severn Valley Railway for its spring gala in 2013, West Country Pacific No. 34007 *Wadebridge* crosses Oldbury Viaduct soon after leaving Bridgnorth on March 31, 2013. ALAN CORFIELD

ABOVE: West Country Pacific 21C123 *Blackmoor Vale* departs from Sheffield Park on the Bluebell Railway on May 13, 1979.

RIGHT: In BR livery, West Country Pacific No. 34023 *Blackmore Vale* is seen at Horsted Keynes on July 25, 1984.

West Country Pacific
No. 21C123 *Blackmoor Vale*
on shed at Sheffield Park
with Merchant Navy
No. 35005 *Canadian Pacific*.
DON BENN

West Country Pacific No. 21C123 *Blackmoor Vale*

West Country Pacific No. 21C123 *Blackmoor Vale* was built at a cost of £17,160 and entered traffic in February 1946. In April 1950 when based at Salisbury, the name was altered to *Blackmore Vale*.

With the impending end of steam on British Railways in July 1967, a group of drivers and their colleagues from Nine Elms, had formed the Bulleid Preservation Society to purchase a Bulleid Pacific. Though not one of the original choices of engine, No. 34023, *Blackmore Vale* and No. 34102, *Lapford* were the only unrebuilt Bulleid Pacifics remaining in traffic at the end and the former was considered to be the most mechanically sound.

On withdrawal and purchase, No. 34023 moved almost immediately to the Longmoor Military Railway, arriving on August 13, 1967, but that centre collapsed and it was moved by road to the Bluebell Railway on October 29, 1971.

Five years later, in May 1976, 21C123, *Blackmoor Vale* entered traffic on the Bluebell Railway, resplendent in SR malachite green livery, the first original Bulleid Pacific to steam in preservation and one of the highlights of the preservation scene in the mid-1970s.

21C123 has been unique in being the only Bulleid Pacific to have carried Southern Railway livery in preservation but it was repainted in BR Brunswick green in 1984, its final BR livery, with additional cosmetic work being undertaken to give the locomotive its 1967 appearance. The locomotive has had a further overhaul and another 10 years in traffic but is currently stored awaiting its next one which will involve major boiler repairs. It has never been seen away from the Bluebell Railway.

BELOW: No. 21C123 running as *OVS Bulleid* and LNER V2 2-6-2 No. 60800 *Green Arrow* depart from Horsted Keynes southbound on October 26, 2003.

ABOVE: En route for its new but short-lived career working for Wessex Trains on the Southern Region, Battle of Britain Pacific No. 34067 *Tangmere* passes Water Orton on March 22, 2003.

OPPOSITE RIGHT: Battle of Britain Pacific No. 34067 *Tangmere* departs from Haywards Heath with the Railway Touring Company's 'Bath & Bristol' tour from Three Bridges on March 19, 2011.

Battle of Britain Pacific No. 34067
Tangmere

Named after a military airfield in Sussex, 21C167 *Tangmere* was completed at Brighton works in September 1947.

During its time in service, *Tangmere* worked out of sheds at Stewarts Lane, Battersea and Salisbury, although its final transfer was to Exmouth Junction where it was almost immediately condemned.

After covering nearly 700,000 miles, *Tangmere* was withdrawn from service on November 16, 1963, and in April 1965 was moved to Woodham's scrapyard at Barry. *Tangmere* moved to the Mid-Hants Railway for restoration on January 24, 1981, however most of the restoration took place at Riley & Sons Engineering Company's works at Bury in Lancashire.

Early in 2003, owned by the late Brian Pickett, *Tangmere* was returned to steam on the East Lancashire Railway and returned to main line running on March 1. Although it failed at Oxenholme on the West Coast Main Line, it was destined to become a regular performer throughout the country.

Its owner assembled a set of Mk.2 stock and marketed railtours in the south of England under the Wessex Trains banner, based at Old Oak Common, but following his death, the company folded and *Tangmere* came into the ownership of Ian Riley, operating on the main line under West Coast Railways of Carnforth. It was subsequently sold again to become a permanent member of the West Coast fleet, normally based at Southall, and remains in frequent use on railtours mainly on the Southern Region but many other unusual locations as well.

Battle of Britain Pacific No. 34067 *Tangmere* departs from Bury on the East Lancashire Railway on January 25, 2004.

7P 5FA

34067

TANGMERE
BATTLE OF BRITAIN CLASS

On November 26, 2011, Battle of Britain Pacific No. 34067 *Tangmere* becomes the first Bulleid Pacific to be seen at Euston since 1948. ANDREW PM WRIGHT

RIGHT: No. 34067 *Tangmere* drops down the gradient past Battersea power station into Victoria with Kingfisher Railtours' 'Statesman' on the evening of July 16, 2006. GEOFF SILCOCK

BOTTOM: With a train of green coaches in tow, No. 34067 *Tangmere* climbs the 1-in-80 of Buriton bank out of Rowlands Castle on the Portsmouth direct line with Steam Dreams' 'Southern Phoenix', July 7, 2007, the 40th anniversary of the end of Southern steam. WARWICK FALCONER

BELOW: No. 34067 in Folkestone Warren with the 9.05 Victoria to Folkestone Harbour on January 27, 2007. DON BENN

ABOVE: No. 34067 *Tangmere* takes the Salisbury line and passes under Battledown flyover which carries the Southampton line which diverges at Worting Junction. JOHN TITLOW

Battle of Britain Pacific No. 34051 *Winston Churchill*

The first of the Battle of Britain class of light Pacifics, 21C151, was built at Brighton works in 1946 and released to traffic on December 30 that year, initially unnamed. It was first allocated to Salisbury.

It was named *Winston Churchill* in a ceremony at Waterloo station on September 11, 1947. The former Prime Minister, by then Leader of the Opposition, was offered the chance to name the locomotive, but turned it down, claiming a prior engagement. It was eventually named by Lord Dowding, who also named 'his' locomotive, No. 21C152, at the same ceremony.

On January 24, 1965, Sir Winston Churchill died, and his state funeral on January 30, 1965, saw his coffin carried from Waterloo on a special train to Handborough, Oxfordshire, hauled by No. 34051.

No. 34051 was withdrawn later that year on September 19, but had been chosen as the representative of Bulleid's Pacific design for the National Collection. It fortunately still remains in original condition.

Withdrawn later than other SR National Collection engines, there was no room at Stratford and No. 34051 went first to Hellifield but joined the others at Preston Park on October 27, 1967.

It was loaned to the Great Western Society at Didcot in October 1977 for static display, not far from Winston Churchill's last resting place at Bladon, but remained in as withdrawn condition.

After transfer to the NRM at York in 1983, it was finally given a coat of paint, and it has been seen on display at various locations, but there have never been any plans to steam it.

In 2013, the National Railway Museum announced that an appeal launched by the Friends of the National Railway Museum in January 2011 to raise the money to give *Winston Churchill* a new look in time for 2015, the 50th anniversary year of the wartime leader's death, had reached the halfway point, and work was due to start on the engine at Ropley. The locomotive had remained in much the same condition it arrived in, and was in urgent need of a cosmetic overhaul.

Battle of Britain Pacific No. 34051 *Winston Churchill* in as withdrawn condition at Didcot on March 1, 1979.

Battle of Britain Pacific No. 34051 *Winston Churchill* in the National Railway Museum at York.
ROBIN JONES

ABOVE: Bulleid Battle of Britain Pacific No. 34070 *Manston* at Corfe Castle with a Matt Allen/Warwick Falconer photo charter on the Swanage Railway on March 8, 2010. PAUL BLOWFIELD

BELOW: Bulleid Battle of Britain Pacific No. 34070 *Manston* heads south from Corfe Castle on the Swanage Railway. PETER ZABEK

Battle of Britain Pacific No. 34070 *Manston*

21C170 *Manston* was the last Bulleid Pacific to be built for the Southern Railway, emerging from Brighton in November 1947 and working initially from Ramsgate. With the Kent Coast lines electrified, *Manston* moved to Exmouth Junction from where it was withdrawn in August 1964.

It was the 146th locomotive rescued from Barry scrapyard, purchased by the Manston Locomotive Preservation Society and on June 3, 1983, arrived at a site at Richborough power station in Kent. Closure of the site led to a move to the Great Central Railway on March 23, 1996.

The society joined the Southern Locomotives Group and the engine was moved to its base at Sellindge, Kent, where restoration work was accelerated and it entered service on the Swanage Railway on September 14, 2008, becoming a regular performer on the line, but making occasional visits to other railways.

On its first day back in service, Bulleid Battle of Britain Pacific No. 34070 *Manston* pilots West Country No. 34028 *Eddystone* out of Corfe Castle on the Swanage Railway on September 14, 2008. ANDREW PM WRIGHT

No. 34072 awaits restoration at Blunsdon on the Swindon & Cricklade Railway.

No. 34072 *257 Squadron* along with West Country No. 34105 *Swanage* and M7 0-4-4T No. 30053 on shed at Swanage on March 19, 1993.

Battle of Britain Pacific No. 34072
257 Squadron

Built by BR at Brighton in 1948, No. 34072 was initially allocated to Dover but moved on to Exmouth Junction in 1958, where it stayed until transferred to Eastleigh in July 1964 from where it was withdrawn in October that year.

A group which was already involved in overhauling Merchant Navy No. 35027 *Port Line*, purchased No. 34072 and moved it initially to the Swindon & Cricklade Railway at Blunsdon in 1985. On November 18, 1987, the locomotive was moved to the former Swindon works weighbridge along with *Port Line*.

In 1988, the group was offered an interest free loan by Tarmac Ltd which enabled three people to be employed full time to complete the restoration of No. 34072 in time for the 50th anniversary of the Battle of Britain on September 15, 1990, which 257 Squadron had been involved in. Despite time-consuming moves within the one-time works complex, restoration work progressed well.

BR Network SouthEast invited the locomotive to attend a celebration at Folkestone and there were plans to haul shuttles on the Folkestone Harbour branch. Although No. 34072 did not

257 Squadron carries the 'Golden Arrow' embellishments.

work the shuttles, it did make a short run on the main line at Folkestone, although it proved to be a big challenge to complete the locomotive in time, and it unexpectedly had to travel to Folkestone by road, causing a 20-vehicle pile-up while waiting on the hard shoulder of the M25 as motorists slowed to look at it.

The renaming ceremony on September 8 was performed by Air Commodore Peter Brothers, a former pilot in the squadron, and an air display featured a Spitfire flypast.

No. 34072 was not destined for a main line career though and moved immediately to the Bluebell Railway, the Swanage Railway in November and the North Yorkshire Moors Railway in April 1991. October that year saw it move to the East Lancashire Railway, returning to Swanage 12 months later. Its 10 year boiler certificate saw it working hard to earn its keep but it retired in early 2003 and now requires a further overhaul.

No. 34072 *257 Squadron* pilots West Country No. 34105 *Swanage* away from Swanage past M7 0-4-4T No. 30053 on March 19, 1993.

Battle of Britain Pacific No. 34073 *249 Squadron*

21C173 *249 Squadron* was one of the last Bulleid Pacifics to leave Barry scrapyard, on February 21, 1988, by then in deplorable condition, as part of a scheme to set up a steam centre in the one-time Pullman car works at Preston Park, Brighton. Once there, little was ever achieved, and getting the engines out proved even more problematical than getting them in. It briefly moved to Swindon but arrived at Ropley on the Mid Hants Railway in April 1994.

In 2006 the locomotive left the Mid-Hants in order to donate parts of its valve gear to sister engine No. 34067 *Tangmere*, which had suffered a catastophic failure while hauling a main line excursion, causing its valve gear oil bath to be punctured.

After a period of storage at Riley & Son Engineering Co's works at Bury, *249 Squadron* moved to Carnforth in January 2014.

Battle of Britain Pacific No. 34073 *249 Squadron* at Ropley on the Mid-Hants Railway on January 9, 1996.
KEN LIVERMORE

RIGHT: Battle of Britain
Pacific No. 34081 *92
Squadron* on November 27,
1976, after arrival at
Wansford on the Nene Valley
Railway for restoration.

BELOW: No. 34081 arrives at
the Nene Valley Railway's
Wansford station in 1998.

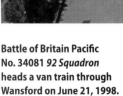

Battle of Britain Pacific
No. 34081 *92 Squadron*
heads a van train through
Wansford on June 21, 1998.

Battle of Britain Pacific No. 34081 *92 Squadron*

No. 34081 *92 Squadron* entered service on September 10, 1948, after Nationalisation, in malachite green livery but carrying a BR number and initially allocated to Ramsgate.

It was named without ceremony in April 1950 after the famous Spitfire squadron based at Biggin Hill during the Battle of Britain in 1940.

Made redundant by the Kent electrification scheme, No. 34081 was reallocated in September 1957 to Exmouth Junction, but worked from Eastleigh from 1964 until withdrawal in August.

On April 2, 1965, it was taken in convoy with Nos 34058, 34067 and 34073 to Woodham's scrapyard at Barry, South Wales, by No. 34006. Purchased from Barry by the Battle of Britain Locomotive Preservation Society, it arrived at the British Sugar Corporation sidings at Peterborough on November 8, 1976, from where it was towed by a Barclay 0-4-0ST to Wansford, on the Nene Valley Railway, where restoration commenced.

Restoration took 22 years to complete, but on March 9, 1998, No. 34081 moved under its own power for the first time in 34 years, with the society's CME, Alan Whenman on the regulator and Charlie Young firing.

No. 34081 headed its first revenue earning passenger train on May 28, and was officially named *92 Squadron* by Pete Waterman and rededicated at 10am with Oliver Bulleid, a grandson of the designer, present.

92 Squadron was a regular performer on the Nene Valley Railway, even hauling Santa specials of air-braked continental stock, and made visits to the Bluebell, Swanage, Mid-Hants and North Yorkshire Moors railways. A move to the North Norfolk Railway took place in 2007, where earning potential was considered greater, as some expensive boiler repairs had to be undertaken. On expiry of the boiler certificate however, the engine returned to Wansford, a more accessible restoration base for society volunteers.

Battle of Britain Pacific No. 34081 *92 Squadron* departs from Corfe Castle on the Swanage Railway on July 8, 2007 during the 40th anniversary of the end of Southern steam gala.

In BR Brunswick green livery, Battle of Britain Pacific No. 34081 *92 Squadron* approaches Holt on the North Norfolk Railway on August 31, 2007.

Battle of Britain Pacific No. 34081 *92 Squadron* heads along the North Norfolk coast near Sheringham on September 19, 2004.

West Country Pacific No. 34092
City of Wells

Fifty West Country Pacifics were built, followed by 40 Battle of Britains; the next 18 reverted to West Country names rounded off by two more Battle of Britains. No. 34092 *City of Wells* was one of the first of the second batch of West Countries. It was named at a ceremony in the city in November 1949, which necessitated strengthening the track on the branch to Wells, and worked from Stewarts Lane for the first 11 years of its life.

It was the first of the Bulleid Pacifics to be purchased from Barry scrapyard, by Rochdale solicitor Richard Greenwood, already owner of USA 0-6-0T No. 30072. The Pacific was also destined for the Keighley & Worth Valley Railway, arriving on October 27, 1971.

Being in relatively good condition by comparison with later purchases, restoration by volunteers took only eight years and No. 34092 headed its first train up the 1-in-58 gradients of the five mile Midland Railway branch in the unlikely surroundings of West Yorkshire in October 1979.

The following year it saw fairly regular use but at the end of the season it was moved to the Steamtown museum and engineering works at Carnforth amid talk of a possible main line debut. BR was reticent over the use of engines with the unusual features of a Bulleid Pacific, but nevertheless, the work required

to upgrade the engine was carried out and on November 28, 1981, *City of Wells* hauled a 'Cumbrian Mountain Express' from Carnforth to Hellifield, the first 'Spamcan' on the main line for 14 years.

Later fitted with a Giesl ejector, following the precedent set by No. 34064 *Fighter Command, City of Wells'* performances were spectacular. Regular work continued, on the Settle & Carlisle, Cumbrian Coast and York-Scarborough routes, and in July 1988, No. 34092 made a welcome return to Southern metals, heading the 'Blackmore Vale Express' between Salisbury and Yeovil Junction, allegedly touching 93mph in the process.

The boiler certificate expired in 1988 and No. 34092 retired for overhaul, which has so far taken 25 years, but the engine had a steam test at Haworth in early 2014.

RIGHT: In steam for its first loaded test run on the Keighley & Worth Valley Railway after restoration, West Country Pacific No. 34092 *City of Wells* stands at Oxenhope on October 7, 1979.

BELOW: West Country Pacific No. 34092 *City of Wells* passes Kettlesbeck Bridge near Clapham, North Yorkshire, returning to York from Carnforth on August 6, 1988.

LEFT: West Country Pacific No. 34092 *City of Wells* departs from Keighley on August 24, 1980.

TOP: West Country Pacific No. 34105 *Swanage* at Barry scrapyard on March 10, 1973.

ABOVE: No. 34105 *Swanage* at Ropley shed on the Mid-Hants Railway on December 5, 1987.

West Country Pacific No. 34105 *Swanage*

No. 34105 *Swanage* was built by BR at Brighton in 1950 and spent most of its working life allocated to Bournemouth, but was quickly condemned after being transferred to Eastleigh in September 1964.

It was rescued from Barry, arriving on the Mid-Hants Railway in March 1978 and returning to steam in August 1987. It has paid working visits to the West Somerset, Great Central and Swanage railways, but is now undergoing major overhaul in Ropley works.

The boiler of No. 34105 undergoing heavy overhaul in Ropley works in 2013.
JAMES HAMILTON

West Country Pacific No. 34105 *Swanage* departs from Alresford on the Mid-Hants Railway with a Santa special on November 27, 1987.

CHAPTER 11

Rebuilding of the Bulleid Pacifics

The unconventional Pacifics started to look more conventional in the 1950s.

By 1948, standardisation was the name of the game in railway motive power circles. GWR steam engines were very much standardised after 1923, if rather different to those on other railways. Ivatt and Fairburn continued Stanier's process of standardisation on the LMS, with Royal Scots and Patriot 4-6-0s being converted to taper boilers and the Princess Coronation Pacifics being de-streamlined. Thompson tried to rebuild Gresley's designs on the LNER with varying degrees of success, and much of this work, influenced by wartime operating conditions, continued on the Western, London Midland, Eastern, North Eastern and Scottish regions of British Railways.

There were two logical next steps; under different circumstances, we could easily have seen the LNER A4s de-streamlined and the A3s and A4s converted to conventional three-cylindered engines, instead of having Gresley's conjugated valve gear. Thompson would no doubt have done this and Stanier is known to have favoured the idea, but the A3s were still being upgraded from the original A1 design and all LNER Pacifics were receiving double chimneys, so to further rebuild engines already in the process of rebuilding would have been a little uneconomical. What stood out though were the Bulleid Pacifics.

The powers-that-be felt that the good points of Bulleid's Pacific design could be retained and enhanced in an engine of more conventional design.

The Merchant Navy Pacifics were considered the priority for rebuilding, and the first one, No. 35018 *British India Line,* emerged in 1955, to a design by R G Jarvis. Gone was the chain-driven valve gear, which had not been a total success, and the troublesome steam reverser; but, most strikingly, gone was the air-smoothed casing. The superb boiler could not be improved on though, and remained untouched, if rather more visible.

There was a clear BR Standard influence in the rebuilt Bulleid Pacifics, but beyond the high running plate and smoke deflectors, any similarity with Riddles' Britannia Pacifics disappeared. This was still a Class 8 three-cylindered express Pacific. Already considered good engines, the railway infrastructure was recovering from the war years and with better maintenance, Bulleid's Pacifics were

now getting the opportunity to prove that they could be exceptional. The boiler is regarded as probably the most free-steaming of all British Class 8 designs, the three-cylinder layout is more economical to maintain than four, but without the inherent problems of Gresley's conjugated valve gear layout.

The Merchant Navies tend to be associated with the LSWR routes from Waterloo but in the 1950s were also in charge of the heavier trains to the Kent Coast, these lines having finally had their axle loading increased. Electrification was planned here though.

The last Merchant Navy was rebuilt in 1959, and work started on the Light Pacifics. Sixty of the 110 locomotives were rebuilt between 1957 and 1961, the first being No. 34005 *Barnstaple.* Retaining the huge and ornate nameplates, often with a crest or coat of arms, the West Countries and Battle of Britains, now visually identical to the Merchant Navies in rebuilt form, were very smart and impressive machines and were to bring the era of steam hauled express train travel in Britain to a close in only another 10 years' time.

The rebuilding solved most of the maintenance problems while retaining the positive features of the original design. Repair costs were reduced by up to 60%, and coal consumption was reduced by up to 8.4%. However, the Walschaerts valve gear made the rebuilds heavier and more prone to hammerblow on the track. The increased weight reduced their route availability and they could not be used on certain routes such as the line to Ilfracombe.

There was little, if any, loss in performance, and there are several authenticated examples of the rebuilt Merchant Navies exceeding the magic 'ton' - No. 35003 *Royal Mail* topping 106mph with a Weymouth-Waterloo service between Basingstoke and Woking just two weeks before the end of SR steam.

The SR was the last main line in the UK to operate express services with steam: the Waterloo-Southampton-Bournemouth-Weymouth expresses remaining almost exclusively Bulleid-Pacific hauled right to the end. Appropriately, it fell to the last Merchant Navy, No. 35030 *Elder-Dempster Lines,* to haul the very last steam-hauled train to Waterloo: the 2.11pm from Weymouth on July 9, 1967. The next day, modern traction took over.

Three rebuilt Bulleid Pacifics meet as West Country No. 34101 Hartland and Merchant Navy No. 35005 Canadian Pacific pass another West Country, No. 34039 Boscastle, on a freight train at Swithland on the Great Central Railway on February 25, 1995.

ABOVE: Rebuilt Merchant Navy No. 35005 *Canadian Pacific* running as No. 35008 and West Country No. 34007 *Wadebridge* are face to face at Ropley during the Mid-Hants Railway's End of Southern Steam 40th anniversary gala in July 2007.

BELOW: Battle of Britain No. 34070 *Manston* in original condition makes an interesting comparison with rebuilt Merchant Navy No. 35005 *Canadian Pacific* at Eastleigh works.

West Country Pacific No. 34016 *Bodmin* departs from Alresford on the Mid-Hants Railway on July 3, 1983.

West Country Pacific No. 34016 *Bodmin*

21C116 *Bodmin* was completed in November 1945 and named by the Mayor of Bodmin at the town on August 28, 1946. It worked from Exmouth Junction until 1958, and then firstly in Kent, being rebuilt in its present form at Eastleigh in April 1956 before being based at Eastleigh for its final years in service from 1961. *Bodmin* was withdrawn in June 1964 and sent to Woodham's scrapyard at Barry in February 1965, having covered more than 800,000 miles in service.

The first rebuilt light Pacific to leave Barry, it was rescued by John Bunch in 1971 and moved to Quainton Road near Aylesbury, now the Buckinghamshire Railway Centre, on July 29, 1972, before moving to the Mid-Hants Railway in November 1976. *Bodmin* re-entered service after completion of its restoration on September 8, 1979, and was renamed, again by the Mayor of Bodmin, two weeks later.

Another overhaul was completed in June 2000 after which *Bodmin* took charge of Daylight Railtours' Green Train main line operations, starting with a run to Salisbury on June 10, breaking new ground for the preservation era with a trip to the extremity of the Withered Arm at Meldon Quarry on September 30.

Bodmin was a regular on the main line until withdrawal from

service for overhaul. A dispute between Mr Bunch and the MHR has meant that a start has not been made and it remains to be seen what the future holds.

No. 34016 *Bodmin* is seen on the Withered Arm at Okehampton on September 30, 2000, on its Daylight Railtours' trip to Meldon Quarry. ROBIN JONES

Looking not dissimilar to when it was first rescued from Barry scrapyard, No. 34016 stands at Ropley in July 2013.

West Country Pacific No. 34010 *Sidmouth*

21C110 *Sidmouth* entered service in September 1945, being withdrawn in March 1965 and despatched to Barry.

It was bought by Graeme Walton-Binns in 1982 and moved to the North Yorkshire Moors Railway. It was moved to Cargo Fleet on Teesside in 1988 but no restoration work was carried out and it moved back to Grosmont in 1996, now in NYMR ownership, after an acrimonious dispute between the owner and the railway.

The Southern Pacific Rescue Group, which was rebuilding No. 34028 *Eddystone* at Sellindge, became part of Southern Locomotives Ltd in 1995 and purchased No. 34010 in 1997 and moved it to Sellindge.

Southern Locomotives Ltd concentrated its operations at Herston on the Swanage Railway and moved No. 34010 there in 2006 but its frames are now at Swanage and its boiler at Bridgnorth.

No. 34016 is seen in 'end of steam' condition at the 40th anniversary gala on the Mid-Hants Railway in July 2007.

No. 34010 at Grosmont on the North Yorkshire Moors Railway. COLOUR-RAIL.COM

West Country Pacific No. 34027 *Taw Valley* emerges from Foley Park tunnel on the Severn Valley Railway on November 26, 1988.

West Country Pacific No. 34027 *Taw Valley*

21C127 *Taw Valley* was completed at Brighton and entered service in April 1946, named after a natural feature of the Devon countryside. Although initially allocated to work out of Ramsgate in Kent, in 1947 *Taw Valley* was moved to Exmouth Junction.

Following its rebuild at Eastleigh in September 1957, the locomotive was allocated to Bricklayers Arms. It continued to work in this area until electrification of the Kent coast line in 1961, and then worked commuter services from Brighton until transferred to Salisbury in 1963.

No. 34027 was withdrawn from service in August 1964 and towed to Woodham's scrapyard in Barry, where it remained until it was purchased by Bert Hitchen and moved to the North Yorkshire Moors Railway in April 1980, followed by a spell at the East Lancashire Railway from November 24, 1982. The restoration was finally completed after a further move to the Severn Valley Railway on August 11, 1985.

Taw Valley was steamed in 1987 and entered main line service as well as working on the SVR and spending a year on the NYMR.

Having been used on shuttle services on the Folkestone Harbour branch in September 1991, No. 34027 made further preservation history the following year. In company with BR Standard 4MT 4-6-0 No. 75069, *Taw Valley* worked shuttle services between Ashord and Hastings as part of Network SouthEast's Ashford 150 celebrations, but at 9.30pm on the Sunday evening,

the Bulleid headed for London Bridge, becoming the first steam train into the terminus since the end of steam on the Central Division in 1964 and the first to work over live third rail lines in London in the preservation era.

It followed this in even more spectacular style by working the first steam train out of Waterloo since 1967, on September 11, 1992, again running after dark, to Bournemouth. It also took the first steam train of the preservation era up the fearsome bank from Exeter St Davids to Exeter Central on September 5, 1993, admittedly assisted by two Class 50 diesels. Fitted with air brakes, it stood in for Merchant Navy No. 35028 on VSOE duties while *Clan Line* was under overhaul.

Its main line duties have also seen No. 34027 conquering Shap and Ais Gill and it spent some time in the maroon livery of the 'Hogwarts Express' as featured in the Harry Potter series of films and novels. It was used to promote the fourth book, Harry Potter and the Goblet of Fire, and hauled a nationwide tour train, as far north as Perth, with the book author J K Rowling herself on the train.

Following sale to a consortium headed by the Diesel Traction Group's Phil Swallow in 2001, *Taw Valley* is currently under overhaul at the Severn Valley Railway but looks unlikely to return to the main line.

West Country Pacific No. 34027 *Taw Valley* passes Abergele with a 'North Wales Coast Express' on August 15, 1989.

RIGHT: West Country Pacific No. 34027 *Taw Valley* on the Folkestone Harbour branch on September 18, 1991.

BELOW: *Taw Valley* departs from Folkestone Harbour station on September 18, 1991, banked by BR Standard 4MT 2-6-4T No. 80080.

In Hogwarts Castle livery, No. 34027 stands at King's Cross in July 2000.
BERT HITCHEN

West Country Pacific No. 34028 *Eddystone*

West Country Pacific No. 34028 *Eddystone* at Eastleigh works during the centenary open weekend in May 2009.

21C128 *Eddystone* emerged from Brighton in April 1946 and started work at Ramsgate. It is perhaps remarkable that it has survived as in May 1964 it became the first Bulleid Light Pacific to be condemned.

It was purchased from Barry and arrived at the Southern Pacific Rescue Group's base at Sellindge in Kent on April 26, 1986, one of the later departures from the yard, and consequently in very poor condition and with no tender. The SPRG was formed by Richard Moffatt and Colin Hebbes after a meeting of the Barry Steam Locomotive Action Group in 1981. It became part of Southern Locomotives Ltd in 1995.

A move to Herston works at Swanage on June 22, 1999, helped accelerate the restoration and on September 29, 2003, *Eddystone* was moved on to the railway for completion, testing and running-in, entering service in the spring of 2004.

In 2006 though, *Eddystone* travelled north for a year's service on the North Yorkshire Moors Railway, where two driving wheel tyres slipped. After repairs on the Bluebell Railway, the engine spent a further year running in Sussex.

Its long-term home remains Swanage apart from short visits to other lines.

West Country Pacific No. 34028 *Eddystone* climbs away from Leekbrook Junction on the Churnet Valley Railway in Staffordshire on November 13, 2010.

ABOVE: No. 34028 *Eddystone* **arrives at Swanage, where Merchant Navy No. 35028** *Clan Line* **awaits departure with a railtour returning to London.**
ANDREW PM WRIGHT

LEFT: West Country Pacific No. 34039 *Boscastle* **passes Swithland on the Great Central Railway with a goods train on February 25, 1995.**

West Country Pacific No. 34039 *Boscastle*

21C139 *Boscastle* entered service on September 16, 1946, based at Stewarts Lane but moved in November 1948 to Brighton. In August 1949 it became the first West Country Pacific to carry BR Brunswick green livery, now numbered 34039.

During the period from 1951 to March 1952, *Boscastle* was based at the Eastern Region depot at Stratford, working in East Anglia as a substitute for new BR Standard Britannia Pacifics withdrawn for repairs.

January 1959 saw its rebuild completed at Eastleigh, followed by allocation to Bournemouth, from where it became the first rebuilt West Country to work on the Somerset & Dorset line on June 19,

1959. Reallocated to Eastleigh in Septermber 1962, No. 34039 was withdrawn in May 1965, having covered 745,000 miles.

It was sent to Barry scrapyard, from where it was bought by James Tawse, who moved it to the Great Central Railway at Loughborough on January 22, 1973, one of the first Bulleid Pacifics to be purchased from Barry.

The Boscastle Locomotive Syndicate was formed in 1986 to widen ownership. It first moved under its own steam on September 7, 1992, and as well as being a GCR regular for many years, it visited the West Somerset and Gloucestershire Warwickshire railways. It was withdrawn for overhaul in June 2000.

Battle of Britain Pacific
No. 34053 *Sir Keith Park*
departs from Bewdley on
the Severn Valley Railway.
MALCOLM RANIERI

Battle of Britain Pacific No. 34053
Sir Keith Park

21C153 was completed in 1947, and allocated to Salisbury, although it moved around the Southern Region working from various sheds during its career.

No. 34053 arrived at Barry scrapyard in March 1966. It was bought by Charles Timms and was moved in 1984 to the site of Hull Dairycoates shed, the restoration base of the Humberside Locomotive Preservation Group, arriving there in November that year.

Mr Timms died in 1992 and No. 34053 was sold to John Kennedy who moved it to the Railway Age at Crewe, where it arrived on October 21 that year. In 1995, a further move took place, to a site at Thingley Junction near Chippenham but no progress was made, and it was resold to Jeremy Hosking as a source of spare parts for No. 34046 *Braunton,* moving to Bishops Lydeard on the West Somerset Railway on January 10, 1997 and on to Williton shortly afterwards.

Although it nearly lost its boiler to *Braunton,* the remains of the engine were sold yet again to Southern Locomotives Ltd, moving to Sellindge on December 28, 2000. Although one of the most hopeless Bulleid restoration projects, it became a priority for Southern Locomotives Ltd in view of the prominent role that Air Vice-Marshall Park had played in the Battle of Britain. Restoration actually took place on parts of the engine at South Coast Engineering at Portland, the South Devon Railway and Crewe Heritage Centre as well as eventually Herston. The boiler even went back to the West Somerset Railway.

Against the odds, No. 34053 was completed in May 2012, but despite the close association between Southern Locomotives Ltd and the Swanage Railway, SLL was now overhauling Bulleid Pacifics faster than the railway could find work for them. *Sir Keith Park* found gainful employment instead on the Severn Valley Railway, entering service in August 2012. A major incident though, occurred on New Year's Day 2014 when a piston detached from the crosshead and smashed through the middle cylinder cover.

The restoration of No. 34053
Sir Keith Park approaches
completion in Herston
works. ANDREW PM WRIGHT

Battle of Britain Pacific No. 34058
Sir Frederick Pile

21C158 was built at Brighton in March 1947 and named after Sir Frederick Pile, General Officer Commanding of Anti-Aircraft Command during the Battle of Britain. It was rebuilt in March 1960 and No. 34058 continued in service until withdrawal in October 1964, when it found its way to Barry.

It was moved from Barry scrapyard to the Avon Valley Railway at Bitton near Bristol in 1986 but the still unrestored engine was moved as a kit of parts to the Mid-Hants Railway for the work to be completed, the last parts arriving on July 29, 2011.

Battle of Britain Pacific No. 34059
Sir Archibald Sinclair

Emerging from Brighton Works in April 1947 and named after the wartime Air Minister, 21C159 initially went to Nine Elms depot, and in 1949 spent some time on the Eastern Region working from Liverpool Street as a trial of Pacifics on this region.

The locomotive spent nearly all its life on the South Western main lines, moving to Exmouth Junction after rebuilding, before moving to Salisbury in January 1965, although it had a brief spell on the Kent lines in 1960-61.

No. 34059 was withdrawn on May 29, 1966, and was sold to

No. 34058 *Sir Frederick Pile* at Bitton on August 20, 1986. KEN LIVERMORE

Woodham Brothers of Barry. It was bought for preservation for £7250 by a group based on the Bluebell Railway, arriving on October 28, 1979, without a tender, most of these having been disposed of by the yard to a local steelworks for use as ingot carriers.

Wednesday, March 4, 2009, saw the first movement of the locomotive under its own steam since withdrawal.

The locomotive is unique in now running with the first 5250 gallon tender to be built in preservation. The design of this tender, with the twin rear ladders and single rectangular filler, was that which superseded the 5250 gallon rebodied tenders in service, but because of the withdrawal of steam were never actually built.

BELOW: Battle of Britain Pacific No. 34059 *Sir Archibald Sinclair* heads the 'Golden Arrow' Pullman dining train away from Sheffield Park on the Bluebell Railway. PETER ZABEK

West Country Pacifics Nos. 34046 *Braunton* and 34028 *Eddystone* join forces on the West Somerset Railway, leaving Blue Anchor on March 22, 2009. DON BISHOP

West Country Pacific No. 34046 *Braunton*

Built at Brighton in 1946, and named *Braunton* in January 1949, 21C146 worked out of Exmouth Junction, Brighton and Bournemouth before withdrawal in October 1965.

It was one of the last Bulleids to be purchased from Barry and was one of the derelict hulks which arrived at the doomed Preston Park project in August 1988.

It moved to the West Somerset Railway in January 1996, purchased by the West Somerset Railway Association, but there were not the resources to restore it and it joined the extensive fleet of engines being assembled by businessman Jeremy Hosking.

Returned to steam in July 2007, No. 34046 worked on the West Somerset Railway and on September 24, 2008, was named by the Mayor of Braunton.

Now owned and operated by Locomotive 34046 Ltd, it spent a considerable time at Riley & Son Engineering at Bury where somewhat extended preparations for main line operation were undertaken, with occasional running on the East Lancashire Railway.

Finally, on Tuesday, July 16, 2013, No. 34046 departed from Bury heading for Carnforth with its support coach, and undertook the customary circuit from Carnforth via Hellifield, Blackburn and Preston, with a train of West Coast Railways' stock, reaching 75mph on the West Coast Main Line.

Pronounced fit, *Braunton* moved south to take up residence at Southall. Its first passenger run was working the return leg from Southampton to Waterloo of the Railway Touring Company's 'Dorset Coast Express' rom Victoria to Weymouth on August 14. Four days later, *Braunton* was in action on the Great Western, working the 'Torbay Express' from Bristol to Kingswear and return, and has settled in to regular main line action, with occasional visits to heritage lines.

RIGHT: No. 34046 at Brighton in 1996. STUART NELHAMS/WSRA

FAR RIGHT: No. 34046 *Braunton* departs from Minehead with its loaded test run on the West Somerset Railway on August 13, 2008. ALAN GRIEVE

During a period of running in, No. 34046 emerges from Nuttall Tunnel on the East Lancashire Railway on April 27, 2013. PHIL JONES

No. 34046 heads towards Wilpshire tunnel on its main line proving run from Carnforth on July 16, 2013. DAVE RODGERS

BELOW: No. 34046 *Braunton* on the return leg of the 'Torbay Express' leaves Kingswear alongside the River Dart on August 18, 2013. ALAN CORFIELD

ABOVE: No. 34046 awaits departure from Bristol Temple Meads with the 'Torbay Express' on August 18, 2013. DON BENN

RIGHT: Making its first appearance at the head of the Venice Simplon Orient-Express Pullmans, *Braunton* speeds through Worplesdon on November 1, 2013. DON BENN

BELOW: *Braunton* visited the Mid-Hants Railway for its spring gala in 2014 and is seen on Wanders Curve heading for Medstead & Four Marks on March 9. NICK GILLIAM

West Country Pacific No. 34101 *Hartland*

No. 34101 *Hartland* is the only surviving light Pacific of the six built at Eastleigh and is the only rebuilt survivor from the second batch of 18 of the West Country class.

Most of its life was spent on passenger services out of London to the Kent ports. It returned to Eastleigh for rebuilding in 1960, and for its last two years of service before withdrawal in July 1966. *Hartland* moved to Barry scrapyard in October 1966, from where Richard Shaw bought the engine and moved it to his factory at Sinfin in

Derby on October 5, 1978. It was moved to the Great Central Railway, partly restored, on March 18, 1991. Restoration was completed in late 1993, and *Hartland* entered traffic in January 1994 with an official launch on April 30, 1994.

The engine had originally been destined for the Peak Rail project and it moved to Matlock in May 1995 for a few months' service before moving on to work on the North Yorkshire Moors Railway, where it was in regular service until withdrawal for overhaul in 2000.

No. 34101 *Hartland* stands at Darley Dale on Peak Rail on May 13, 1995. Although originally purchased for use on this line, this was the only period when it worked there. BRIAN DOBBS

West Country Pacific No. *34101* Hartland climbs the 1-in-49 past Water Ark on the North Yorkshire Moors Railway on April 12, 1998. JOHN WHITELEY

Merchant Navy Pacific No. 35005
Canadian Pacific

Canadian Pacific is the oldest surviving Merchant Navy, built in 1941 at Eastleigh. Numbered 21C5 it was named at Victoria station in March 1942 and started work at Exmouth Junction.

The first of the class to be saved from Barry scrapyard, it arrived at Carnforth for restoration in March 1973. The intention was that it would be part of the main line fleet which then included LNER A3 Pacific No. 4472 *Flying Scotsman*. However the partly restored engine was purchased from Steamtown by Andrew Naish and moved to the Great Central Railway on June 16, 1989, where it was returned to steam, making its first run on October 20, 1990.

A surprise was a repaint into BR 1950 express passenger blue livery, which the Merchant Navies carried in early BR days, but obviously prior to their rebuilding and the livery is therefore not appropriate to the rebuilt examples.

A further move took it to the Mid-Hants Railway in June 1996, with the engine gaining a main line certificate and working from Tyseley for a period. It moved permanently to the MHR on January 29, 2001, where it lost its blue livery after purchase from Andrew Naish by Marcus Robertson, proprietor of new railtour company Steam Dreams, for 'Cathedrals Express' operations.

It was withdrawn from main line service after a serious incident at Paddock Wood on October 19, 2002, when a small tube blew causing injury to footplate staff. Now owned by the MHR, its overhaul commenced at Eastleigh in 2013.

Newly restored to service, Merchant Navy Pacific No. 35005 *Canadian Pacific* crosses Swithland viaduct on the Great Central Railway on December 30, 1990.

In BR blue livery, Merchant Navy Pacific No. 35005 *Canadian Pacific* crosses Gisburn Viaduct with a 'Cumbrian Mountain Express' on May 29, 1999. JOHN WHITELEY

LEFT: No. 35005 *Canadian Pacific* awaits departure from Waterloo with the 11am 'Cathedrals Express' to Winchester on October 17, 2001. DON BENN

OPPOSITE LEFT: *Canadian Pacific* approaches Paddock Wood with a Victoria to Canterbury 'Cathedrals Express' on October 19 2002, the engine failed at Headcorn on this train and had to be withdrawn from main line service. DON BENN

No. 35005 *Canadian Pacific* at North Street on the Mid-Hants Railway on March 3, 2007. NICK GILLIAM

RIGHT: No. 35006 on display at Toddington in the final stages of restoration in May 2013.

BELOW: No. 35006 has yet to steam in preservation but a foretaste of things to come was provided by No. 35005 *Canadian Pacific* when it visited the Gloucestershire Warwickshire Railway in 2007, where it is seen arriving at Winchcombe.
MALCOLM RANIERI

Merchant Navy Pacific No. 35006
Peninsular & Oriental S N Co.

Built at Eastleigh in December 1941, 21C6 was later to be named *Peninsular & Oriental S N Co,* and allocated to Salisbury shed, where it remained based throughout its working life.

All of the Merchant Navies were rebuilt, with Nos. 35006 and 35028 *Clan Line* being the last two examples to undergo modification in 1959.

After withdrawal, No. 35006 was sold to Woodham Brothers' scrapyard at Barry for £3500.

It was purchased by the 35006 Locomotive Society, and moved to Toddington on the Gloucestershire Warwickshire Railway, on March 19, 1983, where restoration commenced.

The engine is expected to steam in the summer of 2014.

Merchant Navy Pacific No. 35009
Shaw Savill

One of a batch of eight whose air-smoothed casings were made of asbestos board, 21C9 *Shaw Savill* was built at Eastleigh in June 1942 and allocated to Salisbury shed.

Shaw Savill was rebuilt in March 1957, withdrawn from service in July 1964 and arrived at Woodham Brothers' scrapyard in Barry in December 1964.

It was one of the last derelict hulks to leave Barry, arriving at Preston Park but moved briefly to Swindon, then to the Mid-Hants Railway in 1994. Acquired by Ian Riley, No. 35009 was moved to Riley & Son Engineering's base at Bury where it is intended eventually to overhaul it for main line use.

RIGHT: No. 35009 at Barry on August 7, 1984.
KEN LIVERMORE

Merchant Navy Pacific No. 35010 *Blue Star*

First based at Salisbury to work trains on the Waterloo to the West of England route, 21C10 *Blue Star* was built at Eastleigh and entered traffic on July 31, 1942. It was later fitted with an experimental hood and then separate smoke deflectors to try to cure the problem of drifting smoke.

In 1950 it was transferred to Nine Elms and was rebuilt during the winter of 1956/57, then transferred to Bournemouth. It also worked from Exmouth Junction and Weymouth before being withdrawn from BR service with a damaged right-hand cylinder in September 1966, having covered a mileage of 1,241,299.

Blue Star was sold for scrap to Woodham Brothers of Barry where it arrived in March 1967. It was purchased by the British Enginemen's Steam Preservation Society without a tender, and moved to a private site near the North Woolwich Old Station Museum on January 10, 1985. Subsequently a snowplough converted from a Schools class 4-4-0 tender was purchased as a base for the missing tender.

The locomotive was moved to the Colne Valley Railway at Castle Hedingham in Essex on April 18, 1996, where it awaits its turn for restoration.

No, 35010 at Castle Hedingham on the Stour Valley Railway. RAY BISHOP

Merchant Navy Pacific No. 35011 *General Steam Navigation*

21C11 *General Steam Navigation* emerged from Eastleigh works in 1944.

Saved from Barry, it first moved to Preston Park, then to Hull and on to the one-time RAF station at Binbrook in Lincolnshire. It has now joined the collection at Sellindge in Kent.

The 35025 Brocklebank Line Association is hopeful for a future four way tie up between the Remembrance line (the Folkestone Harbour branch and station restoration project), the No. 35011 and No. 35025 groups along with the Sellindge steam restoration company headed by Richard Moffatt.

The grand plan is for both No. 35011 and No. 35025 to be restored to main line running condition and to run excursions over the Folkestone Harbour branch. Passengers would then transfer to a period steamer for a cross channel trip to Boulogne and back, then returning to London steam hauled throughout, at the end of the day. Progress is slow and the project appears to have made little headway so far.

No. 35011 at Williton on the West Somerset Railway.
NICK GILLIAM

Merchant Navy Pacific No. 35018 *British India Line*

Entering service in May 1945, 21C18 was built at Eastleigh. It worked from Nine Elms for virtually its entire life. It was chosen as the Southern representative for the 1948 locomotive exchanges, for comparison on SR routes with an LMS Royal Scot and Princess Coronation Pacific and an LNER A4 Pacific. It was the first Merchant Navy to be rebuilt, emerging from Eastleigh in February 1956.

It was purchased from Barry scrapyard in 1980 by Richard Heather and moved to the Mid-Hants Railway where it arrived on March 14. Restoration started and had reached an advanced stage in 2003, when the engine left for South Coast Steam, a company owned by Barry Gambles and incorporated in January 2003, registered along with South Coast Crane Hire in Loughborough, but operationally located in South Coast Crane Hire's main yard in Portland.

The Mid-Hants Railway had served a notice to quit, leading to the move to Portland, but the locomotive is currently under restoration at the West Coast Railway Company's base at Carnforth.

Its overhaul then apparently progressing well, No. 35018 *British India Line* is shunted by Austerity 0-6-0ST No. 196 at Ropley on the Mid-Hants Railway on October 23, 1982. The locomotive however has yet to return to steam. KEN LIVERMORE

Merchant Navy Pacific No. 35027 *Port Line*

The restoration and operation of Bulleid Pacifics, particularly on heritage lines has increasingly come within the auspices of Southern Locomotives Ltd, a company which owns, restores and

No. 35027 *Port Line* at Horsted Keynes. S TROY/ SLL

maintains steam locomotives on a non profit-making basis, all income being ploughed back in the locomotives.

The first project was the restoration of No. 35027 *Port Line*, which was considered by many to be unrestorable, yet which was restored from Barry scrapyard condition in only five years, a timescale never equalled with a locomotive of its size. It was followed by No. 34072 *249 Squadron*, and Southern Locomotives Ltd grew out of these first two ventures.

No. 35027 was moved from Barry scrapyard to Blunsdon on the Swindon & Cricklade Railway on December 18, 1982, and much restoration work took place in the open with very basic facilities.

Tarmac Properties Ltd, offered the group covered accommodation in the weighbridge at the one-time GWR Swindon works and *Port Line* was moved on November 17, 1987.

Returning to steam in February 1988, *Port Line* was based at the Bluebell Railway from May that year until 2000, although its last working on the Bluebell was in 1996. It moved to the Swanage Railway on February 26, 2000, with further boiler work allowing it to operate on a limited basis from November 2000 until October 2003, when firebox cracks forced its withdrawal.

In 2005 though, *Port Line* was sold, as there were insufficient resources to restore it and Merchant Navies are simply too big to work regularly on heritage lines. It became part of Jeremy

Merchant Navy Pacific No. 35022
Holland-America Line

Built at Eastleigh in 1948 and based initially at Exmouth Junction, in 1952, No. 35022 not only took part in trials on the Rugby testing plant but worked test trains including a dynamometer car over the Settle & Carlisle line.

Rescued from Barry, it was moved to the Swanage Railway on March 12, 1986.

The group restoring No. 35022 became part of Southern Locomotives Ltd in 1995, but it was sold by SLL to Jeremy Hosking in 2004, along with No. 35027 *Port Line,* which will be fitted with No. 35022's boiler as part of its overhaul to main line operating condition.

Merchant Navy Pacific No. 35025
Brocklebank Line

No. 35025 entered traffic at Bournemouth shed (71B) on the Southern Region of the newly formed British Railways in November 1948, and was named *Brocklebank Line* at Waterloo by Colonel H E Bates, chairman of the Brocklebank Line Shipping Company.

No. 35025's links with the company have remained to this day as members of the Brocklebank family are active members of the 35025 Brocklebank Line Association. It spent time at a number of sheds including Stewarts Lane, Exmouth Junction and Nine Elms. In December 1956, it was rebuilt. Although one of the last 10 to be built, *Brocklebank Line* was one of the first six to go, being withdrawn in September 1964 at the end of the summer timetable. In November 1964, No. 35025 was sold to Woodham's scrapyard at Barry, arriving there in February 1965.

It was one of three engines earmarked for scrapping but was reprieved by the two week summer break, focusing the minds of people involved in saving it.

Keith Marshall of Oadby, Leicestershire, was already involved in several groups attempting to save Bullied Pacifics from Barry when he was approached to start up a group to rescue No. 35025.

By 1985 enough money had been raised to enable the locomotive to be purchased by the Southern 8P Preservation Group, forerunner of the 35025 Brocklebank Line Association from Dai Woodham, in November 1985 for £8500, moving to the Great Central Railway in February 1986.

By November 1987 with no work started, Brian Seddon as chairman, Michael Wood as secretary and Richard Derry as treasurer took over management of the project, and a substantial amount was achieved.

This halted in the spring of 2005 when a notice to quit the site was issued by the new board of the GCR. After a traumatic period for the group, relocation to Sellindge in Kent was achieved in October/November 2007, but in the meantime someone burgled the 35025 parts store at Loughborough, selecting all of the gunmetal, bronze, brass and copper fittings and material.

ABOVE: Merchant Navy No. 35022 *Holland-America Line* **rests by the bufferstops at Swanage.**
COLOUR-RAIL.COM

OPPOSITE LEFT: A sight which would have been unthinkable for Bluebell pioneers in 1960; No. 35027 *Port Line* **passes under Three Arch Bridge on the approach to Horsted Keynes in September 1988.**
PETER ZABEK

Hosking's fleet, to be overhauled for main line use at Southall, where it arrived in January 2011. Under the ownership of Jeremy's Royal Scot Locomotive and General Trust (RSL&GT), *Port Line* was later moved to Ian Riley's workshops at Bury on the East Lancashire Railway where overhaul to main line standard continues, and will utilise the boiler from No. 35022 *Holland-America Line.*

No. 35025 *Brocklebanl Line's* smokebox and blue-liveried cab at Loughborough on the Great Central Railway on December 31, 1994. KEN LIVERMORE

RIGHT: On its first main line run in preservation, Merchant Navy Pacific No. 35028 *Clan Line* on a Basingstoke - Westbury tour on April 27, 1974.
KEITH JACKSON

BELOW: During its period based at Hereford and working mainly on the Welsh Marches route, Merchant Navy Pacific No. 35028 *Clan Line* departs from Shrewsbury on November 10, 1984.

Merchant Navy Pacific No. 35028
Clan Line

No. 35028 was built at Eastleigh in 1948, allocated at first to Dover then to Stewarts Lane, and was named *Clan Line* on January 15, 1951, by Lord Rotherwick, chairman of the shipping company, at Southampton docks. After rebuilding in 1959 it was initially allocated to Nine Elms. On July 2, 1967, *Clan Line* hauled a farewell special from Waterloo to Bournemouth and back and its last run was on July 5 on the 11.35am Weymouth – Waterloo, from Bournemouth, ending its BR career.

The Merchant Navy Locomotive Preservation Society (MNLPS) was formed at the end of 1965 to preserve a Merchant Navy in working order. A fund of £3850 was raised and No. 35028 was purchased in July 1967 for the sum of £2200. The engine was selected because it had been the most recent member of the class to receive a major repair and had a boiler which was regarded as being in the best condition.

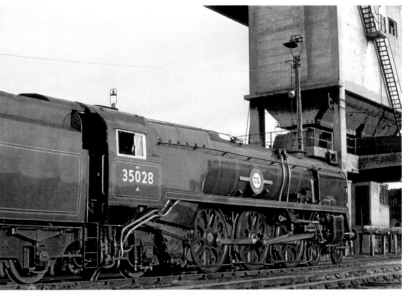

Merchant Navy Pacific No. 35028 *Clan Line* rests by the coaling stage at Carnforth while on 'Cumbrian Coast Express' duties in May 1979.

Matched with Pullman coaches and carrying the 'Golden Arrow' headboard, No. 35028 *Clan Line* takes part in the Rocket 150 cavalcade at Rainhill on August 25, 1980.

During its period based at Marylebone, Merchant Navy Pacific No. 35028 *Clan Line* departs from High Wycombe with a 'Shakespeare Express' to Stratford-upon-Avon.

Finally back in main line action in home territory, Merchant Navy Pacific No. 35028 *Clan Line* departs from Gillingham, Dorset with the 'Blackmore Vale Express', returning from Yeovil Junction to Salisbury on October 11, 1986.

It was delivered to the society on August 13 and moved to the Longmoor Military Railway. The preservation project there floundered and the engine had to be moved, initially to a site a few miles away close to the Waterloo to Portsmouth main line at Liss, but then moved again to the Ashford Steam Centre on August 29, 1971.

Although the operation of privately owned steam engines had been banned by BR in 1967, there was hope of the ban being lifted by this time and it was hoped that *Clan Line* would be selected as suitable for limited BR operation in the future. The plan was to use Ashford as a main line operating base, and with the ban lifted from 1972, a tour of Kent was provisionally arranged, but BR got cold feet over running steam on third rail electrified lines.

Heading the VSOE Pullman train for the first time, Merchant Navy Pacific No. 35028 *Clan Line* departs from Dover on September 24, 1994.

ABOVE: No. 35028 *Clan Line* departs from Waterloo on March 23 1995 with Network SouthEast's 'Ocean Liner Express' to Southampton Eastern Docks. JOHN TITLOW

LEFT: Main line steam at its best: No. 35028 *Clan Line* passes Wimbledon with a VSOE excursion to Southampton Docks on January 17, 2009. KEN WOOLLEY

RIGHT: Approaching completion of its latest overhaul, *Clan Line's* boiler is reunited with its frames at Stewarts Lane on November 11, 2005. RL SEWELL

FAR RIGHT: Hauling timetabled service trains on a heritage line for the first time, *Clan Line* arrives at Medstead and Four Marks on the Mid Hants Railway on March 9 2014. PHIL BARNES

No. 35028 *Clan Line* passes Vauxhall with UK Railtours 'Eastleigh Centenarian' on May 23, 2009.
WARWICK FALCONER

Eventually on April 27, 1974, *Clan Line* hauled its first revenue earning train in preservation from Basingstoke to Westbury, partly on SR metals but keeping well away from electrified lines.

Based at Ashford and only able to run on one route at the opposite end of the Southern Region was not ideal and on April 20, 1975, the Pacific steamed to a new home at the Bulmers Railway Centre at Hereford, joining GWR 4-6-0 No. 6000 *King George V* and LMS Stanier Pacific No. 6201 *Princess Elizabeth*. Gradually more and more of the BR system was opened up to steam and after a few runs on the Welsh Marches route, *Clan Line* was able to run on such lines as the Cumbrian Coast and Settle & Carlisle.

It headed its first train out of a London terminus in preservation in 1985 when it was based at Marylebone from March to haul trains from there to Stratford-upon-Avon and in October 1986 finally made a welcome return to the Southern Region to take part in a series of 'Blackmore Vale Expresses' between Salisbury and Yeovil Junction.

With the prospects of steam operation in the south looking far more favourable, but with no suitable base actually in SR territory, *Clan Line* took up residence in the former GWR shed at Southall in October 1988, and in the early 1990s while the engine was under major overhaul, it was decided to install steam-operated air compressor equipment to enable the operation of air braked trains, the first main line steam locomotive to be fitted in the preservation era.

This decision was made as the vacuum braking system was being phased out by BR. A major bonus was that the air-braked Venice Simplon-Orient-Express Pullman train could now be operated for the first time by steam traction on the main line and the first such train ran in September 24, 1994, hauled by *Clan Line*.

This began a long association with the Orient Express train which continues today, and the opportunity arose of relocating to Stewarts Lane in Battersea where the engine moved in March 1999 to be housed and maintained in a 1950s electric locomotive maintenance building, close to where it had been based for the first 10 years of its working life.

In 2001 the engine was taken out of service for its third major overhaul which took until the end of 2006 to complete before it was once again available for main line use.

Never seriously challenged as the spiritual leader of the Southern steam revival, since it was based on the Longmoor Military Railway in the 1970s, *Clan Line* had been virtually unique in never having hauled any trains on preserved railways but it has made visits to two such lines; the Mid-Hants Railway for some minor work, and the Swanage Railway on railtour duty in 2012. In 2014 though, the Merchant Navy returned to the Mid Hants Railway to take part in its Spring gala weekend and finally made its regular passenger-hauling heritage line debut.

The cutaway side of the boiler, smokebox and cylinders of No. 35029 on display at York.

Merchant Navy Pacific No. 35029
Ellerman Lines

The newest of the surviving Merchant Navies is the least likely to ever steam again.

It was purchased from Barry scrapyard by the National Railway Museum and moved to Market Overton in Rutland in February 1974.

The site here was once a small industrial locomotive shed serving an ironstone quarry but was taken over by William McAlpine's Flying Scotsman Services Ltd with the intention of establishing a base for his engines with a working heritage line.

Here No. 35029 was externally restored but also partially sectioned in order to display the internal workings of a steam locomotive.

Moved to the museum in time for its opening in 1975, it has always proved to be a popular exhibit.

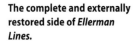

The complete and externally restored side of *Ellerman Lines.*

ABOVE: The sectioned Merchant Navy Pacific No. 35029 *Ellerman Lines* on display at the National Railway Museum at York.

LEFT: The sectioned side of No. 35029 on arrival at the National Railway Museum. .

CHAPTER 13

The Revival Continues

The Southern steam revival is by no means over and continued in 2013 with the two pioneer heritage lines seeing trains on reinstated sections of their respective routes.

The Bluebell Railway revivalists always had thoughts of one day running trains right through to East Grinstead, to connect with the national network, but it has taken a very long time and progress in the 1960s was very definitely backwards with the track being lifted (with the railway's assistance!) and a cutting being filled with domestic refuse. However, BR donated Imberhorne Viaduct to the society in 1992, and acquisition of the then privately owned trackbed continued with the final bit purchased in 2003, allowing a huge civil engineering project to commence.

Fortunately the 3,400,000 cubic feet of waste in the 1600ft-long Imberhorne cutting were found not to be toxic, and work commenced on removing first the topsoil, initially by rail and even steam-hauled, to a site on the old Ardingly spur at Horsted Keynes. On November 25, 1998, BBC newsreader Nicholas Owen, a local resident and Bluebell volunteer, started removal of the actual waste in a public launch of this phase of the project.

Although lorries were used for the actual waste at first, it proved possible, cheaper and more environmentally friendly, to change to rail. With pressure mounting to complete the job quickly because of an imminent increase in landfill tax, a cash target was reached by the society and the rubbish removed by the end of March 2012.

A new station has been built 100 yards south of the national rail station at East Grinstead and work had started in autumn 2008. During the railway's 50th anniversary celebrations in 2010, Dame Vera Lynn launched a £3.8 million appeal to fund the works.

Tracklaying over the four miles from Kingscote was the easy part of the project, with work starting from both ends towards the slowly disappearing tip at Imberhorne. On March 7, 2013, the two sections of track were formally joined using a white fishplate, with the honour of tightening the four bolts being given to Barbara Watkins a long-standing Bluebell Railway volunteer. The official opening of the extension to East Grinstead took place on Saturday, March 23, with a two week opening festival.

A diesel-hauled railtour ran through from London to Sheffield Park shortly afterwards and two steam hauled through trains, both featuring 'foreign' motive power in the shape of *Tornado* and *Oliver Cromwell*, but on November 9, 2013, an ambitious railtour arrived from Victoria having run to Uckfield in the morning. In top and tail fashion, the return run from Sheffield Park to Victoria saw the train headed by recently-restored West Country Pacific No. 34046 *Braunton*. It is even possible that the Bluebell Railway could one day reinstate the line from Horsted Keynes to Haywards Heath.

Rebuilding the Kent & East Sussex Railway beyond Bodiam, to connect with the main line at Robertsbridge will be a major undertaking but tracklaying has continued and in 2013, track was laid at Robertsbridge itself with a 'Terrier' 0-6-0T giving short rides.

The Rother Valley Railway opened in 1900 but its name was changed in 1904 to the Kent & East Sussex Light Railway. It closed to regular passenger services on January 2, 1954, and the Tenterden to Headcorn section was lifted in 1955, but goods trains continued between Robertsbridge and Tenterden until June 1961.

A society was formed in 1961 and the line between Tenterden and Bodiam was purchased, the railway being known as the Kent & East Sussex Railway and opening in stages from 1974, but the preservationists were refused permission by the then Transport Minister Barbara Castle to take over the section onwards from Bodiam to Robertsbridge.

KESR trains finally reached Bodiam on April 2, 2000, and the KESR now has powers to operate as far as Robertsbridge, but had no plans to extend beyond Bodiam. However, a separate company was formed in 1991 to rebuild the 3½ mile Bodiam to Robertsbridge section.

The Rother Valley Railway has been acquiring parts of the trackbed and ¾ mile of track has been relaid at the eastern end, connecting KESR track to Junction Road. At the western end, five bridges have been reconstructed and track laid from the Robertsbridge station area to Northbridge Street.

There is much left to be done as more bridges need reinstating and three level crossings are required, one over the A21 Robertsbridge bypass.

Meanwhile the Swanage Railway progresses with its plans to operate public services right into Wareham. The Lynton & Barnstaple Railway has achieved a lot but its running line is still short. It is making steady progress in acquiring sections of trackbed and safeguarding its route.

The various revival schemes for the much-lamented Somerset & Dorset route should not be overlooked, with progress being seen at several sites.

We may even see further stretches of one time Southern trackage seeing a revival; The Bideford & Instow Railway did operate short distance shuttles but ran into political problems and suspended operations. The site is now the Bideford Railway Heritage Centre, but further down the line, the Tarka Valley Railway received planning permission in 2013 for railway operations based at

LBSCR E4 0-6-2T No. 473 heads through Imberhorne cutting with a train from East Grinstead on the Bluebell Railway on March 27, 2013.
ANDREW STRONGITHARM